Sugar Skulls

Personalities

Day of the dead illustrations

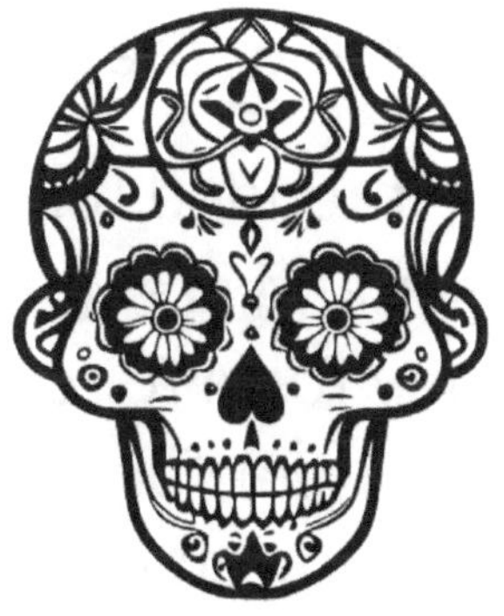

50 sugar skulls to have hours of fun and relaxation

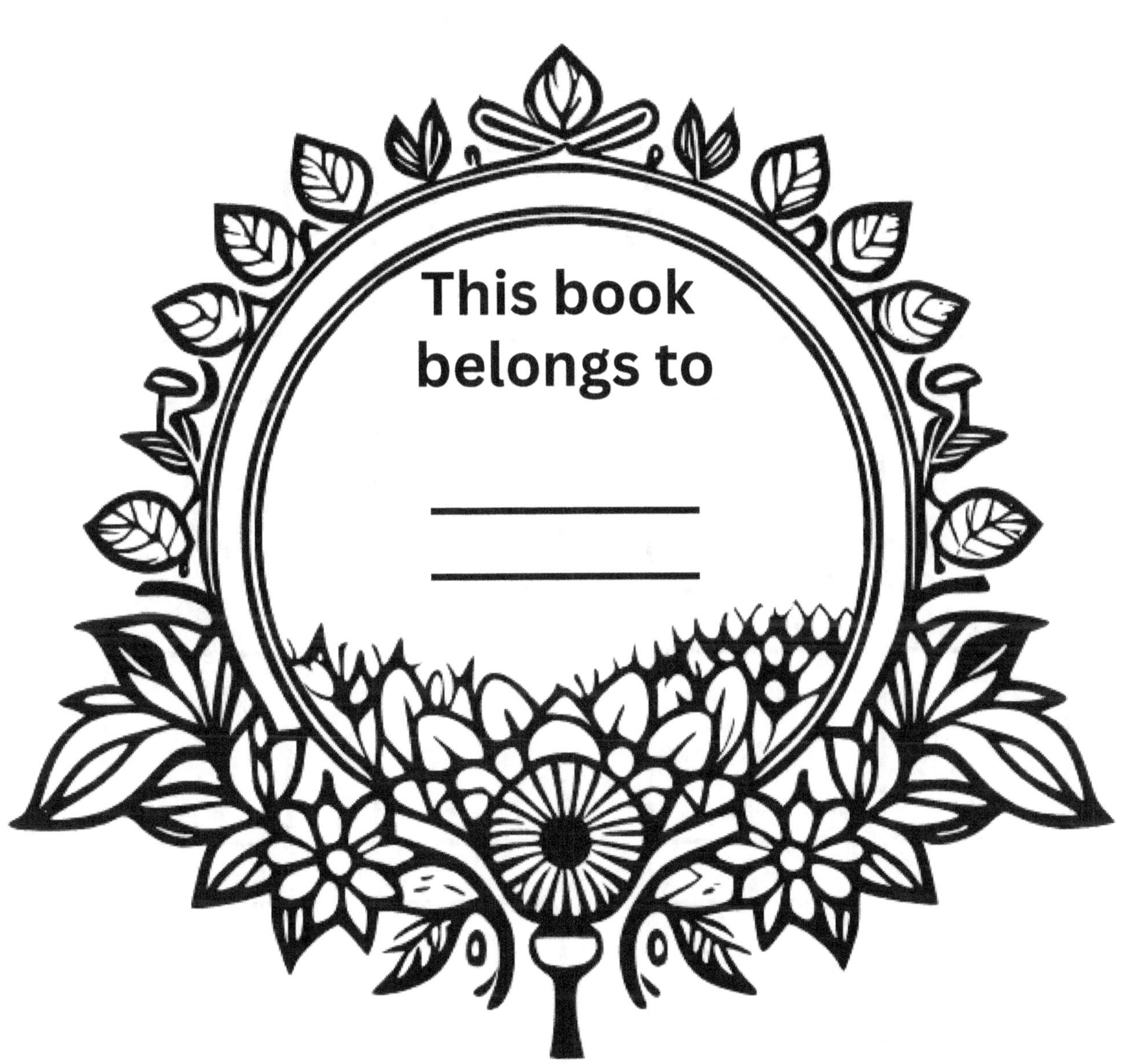This book
belongs to

Test color page

Check how the color show on our page here

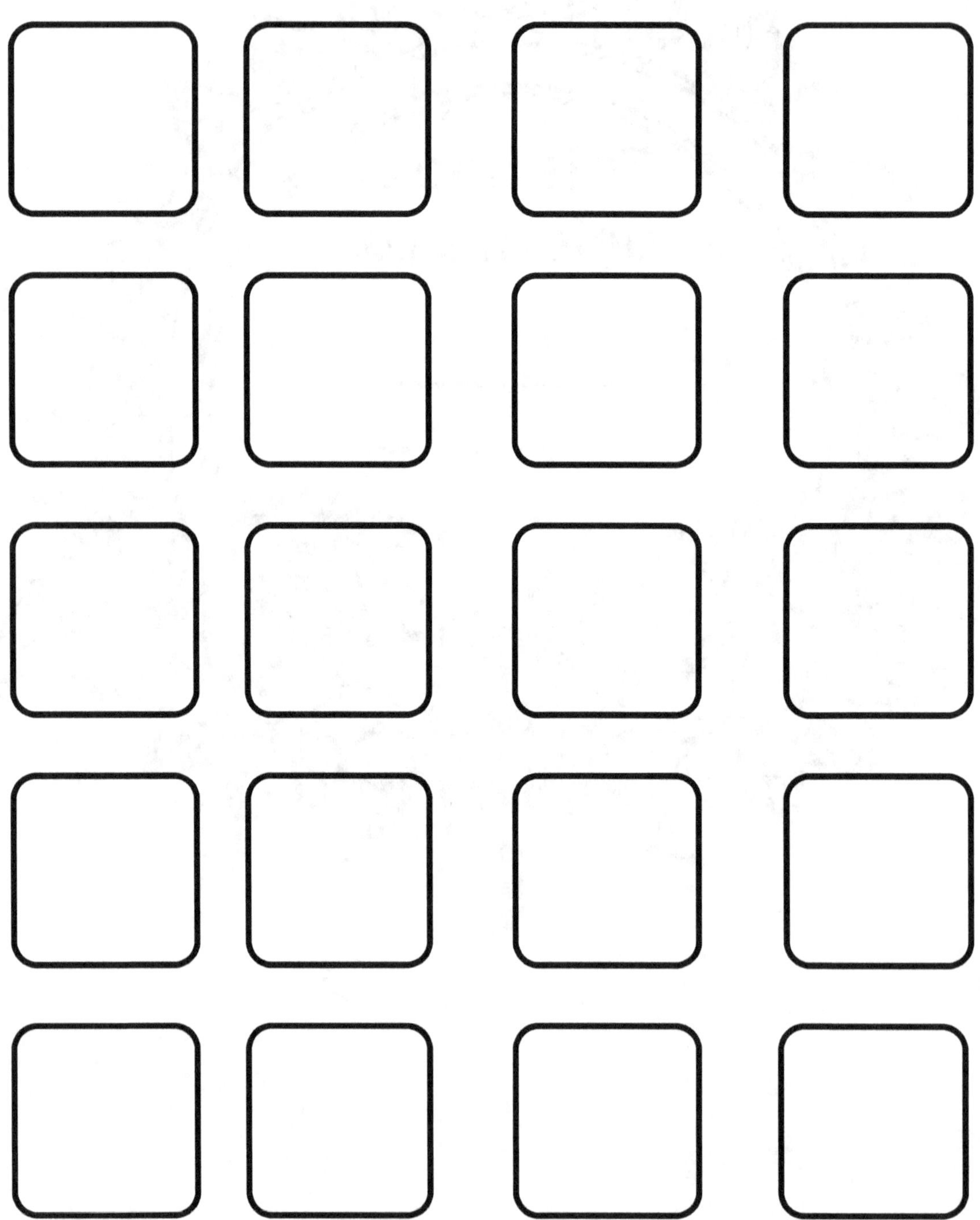

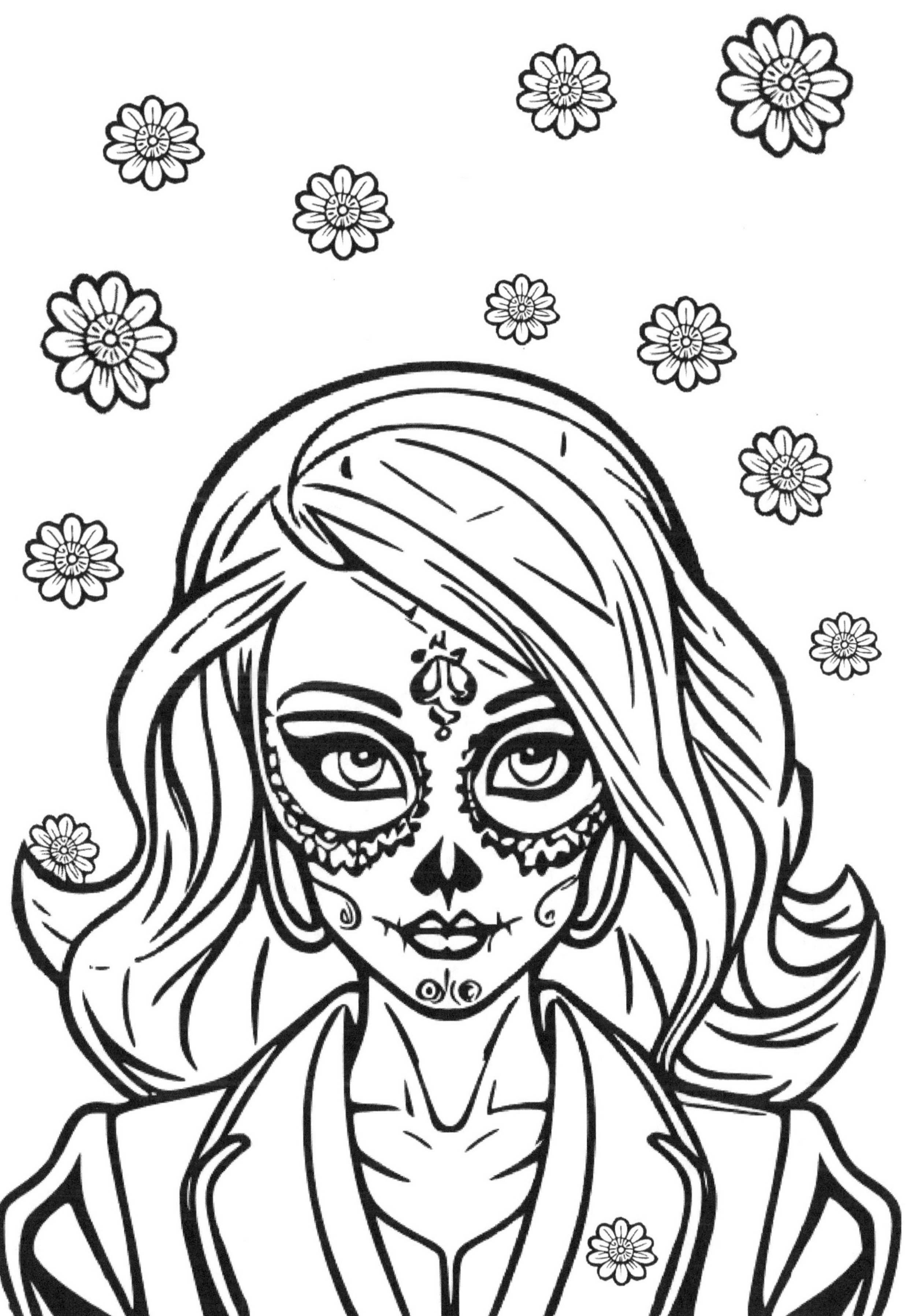

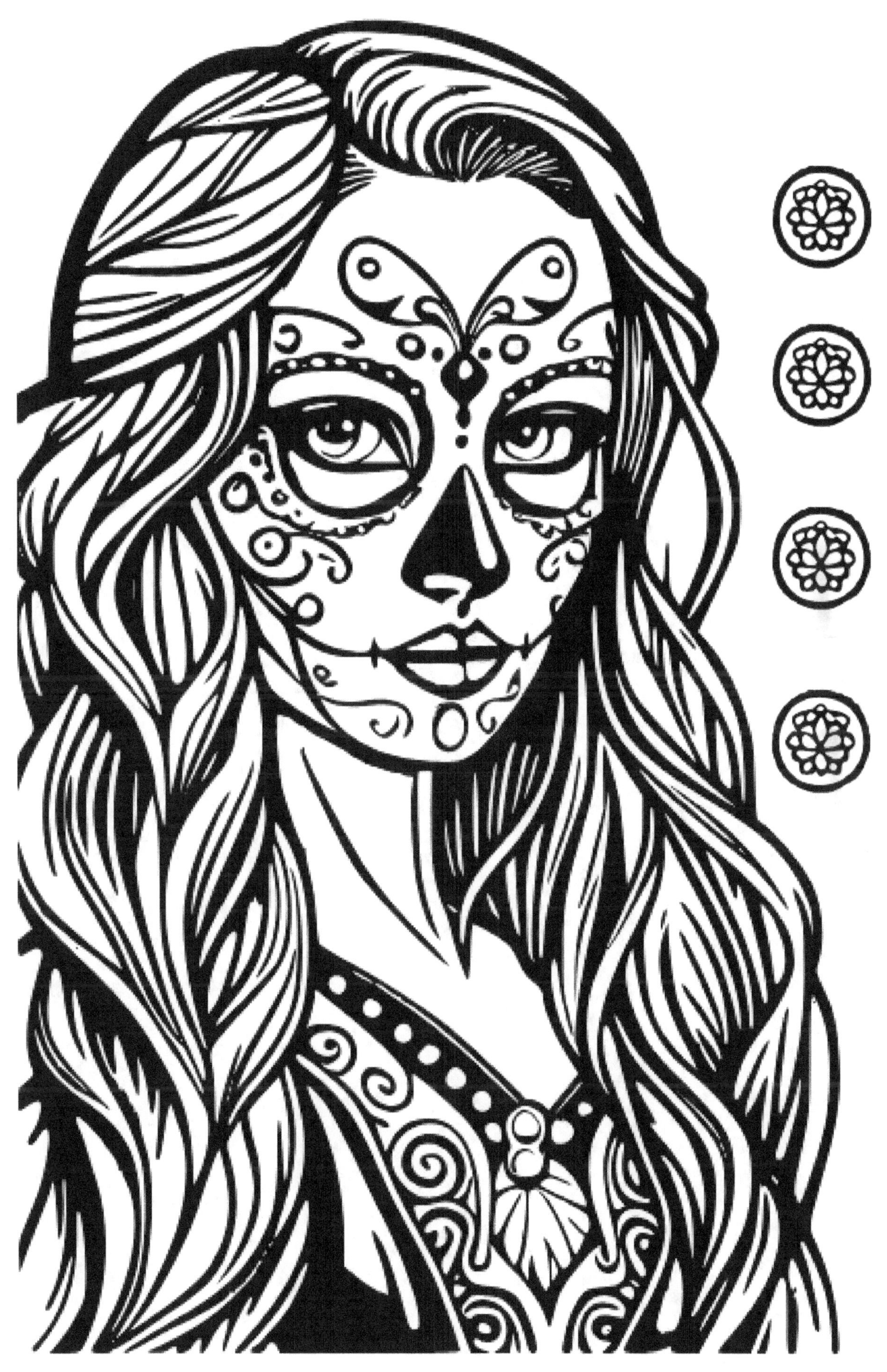

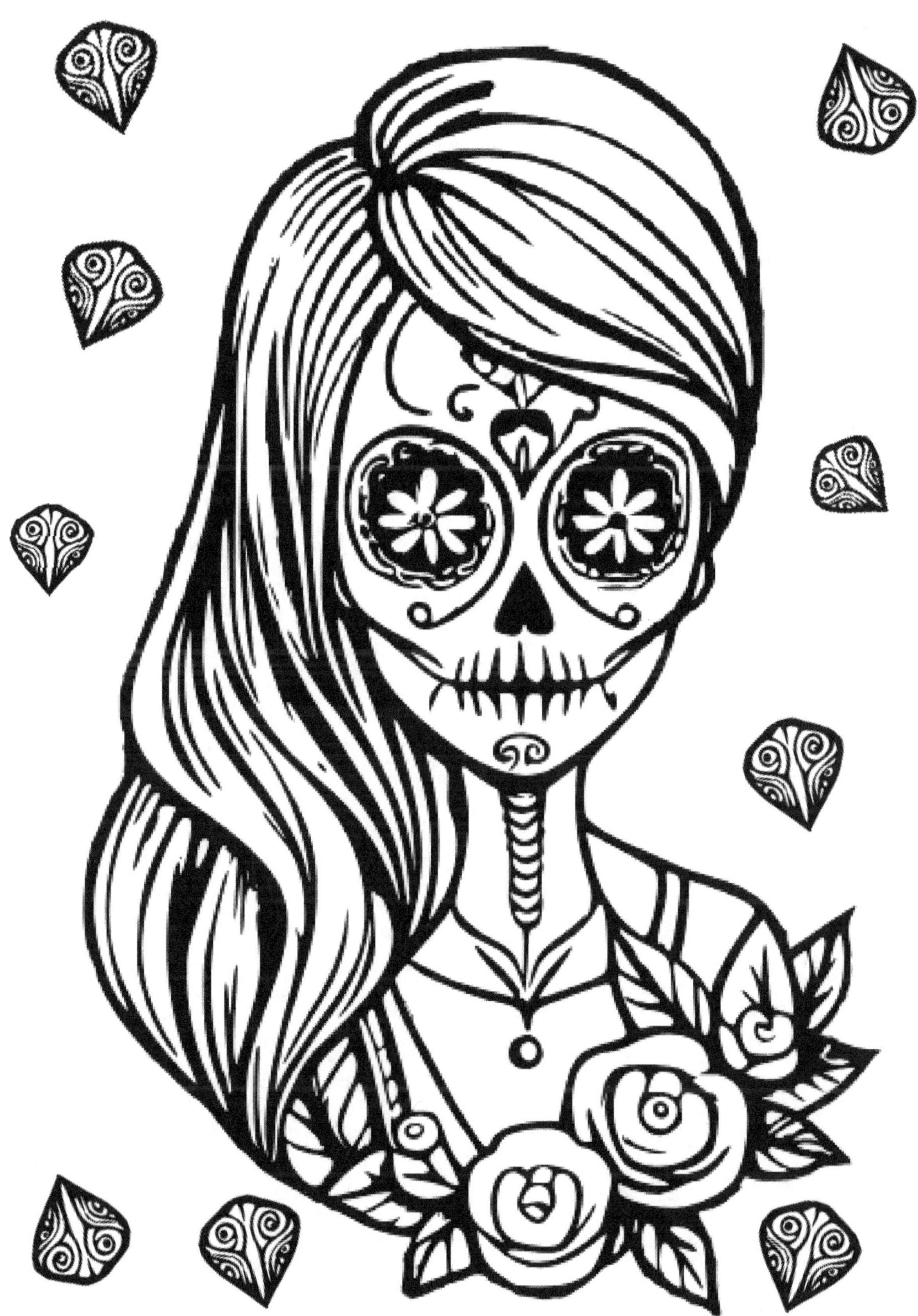

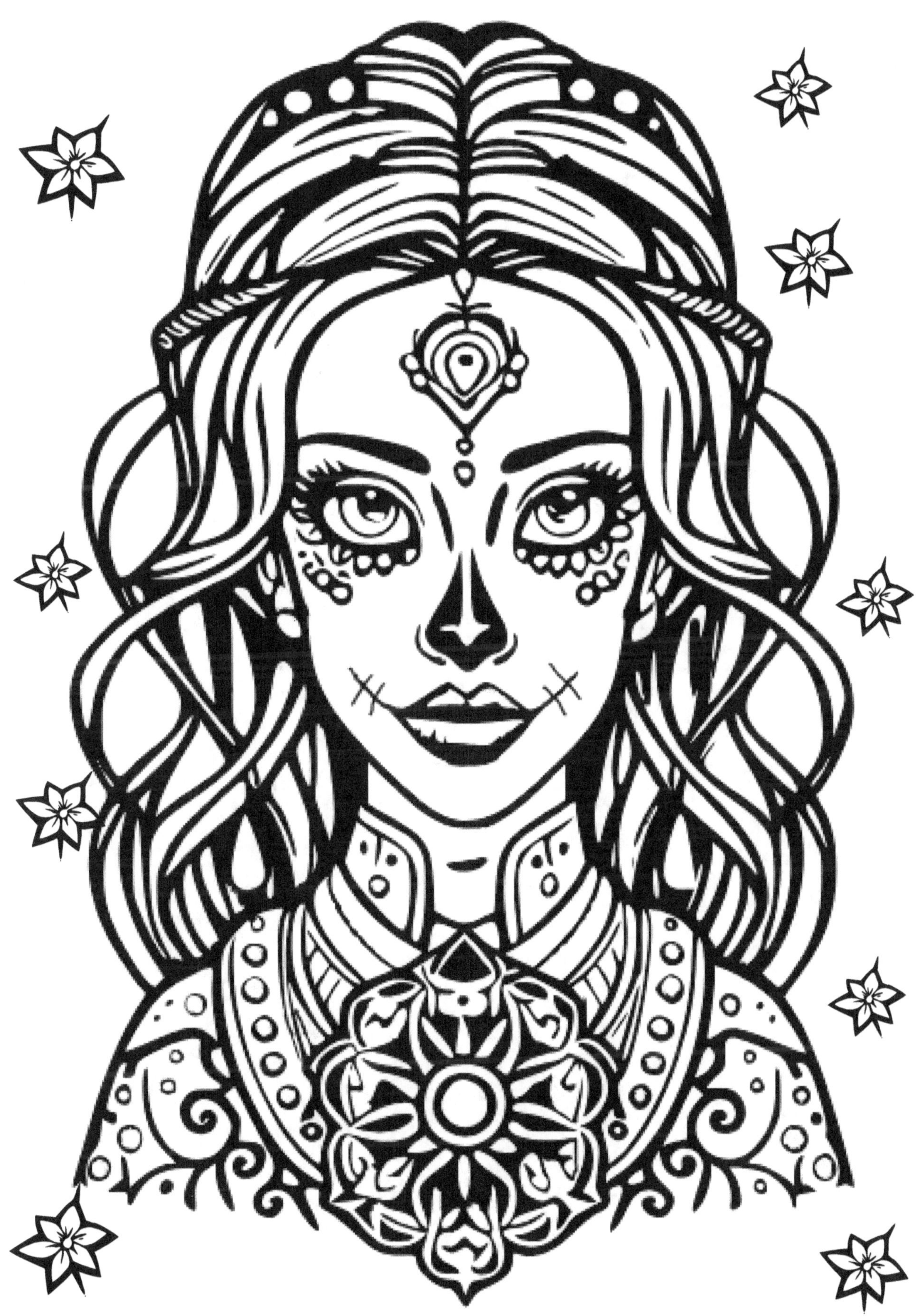

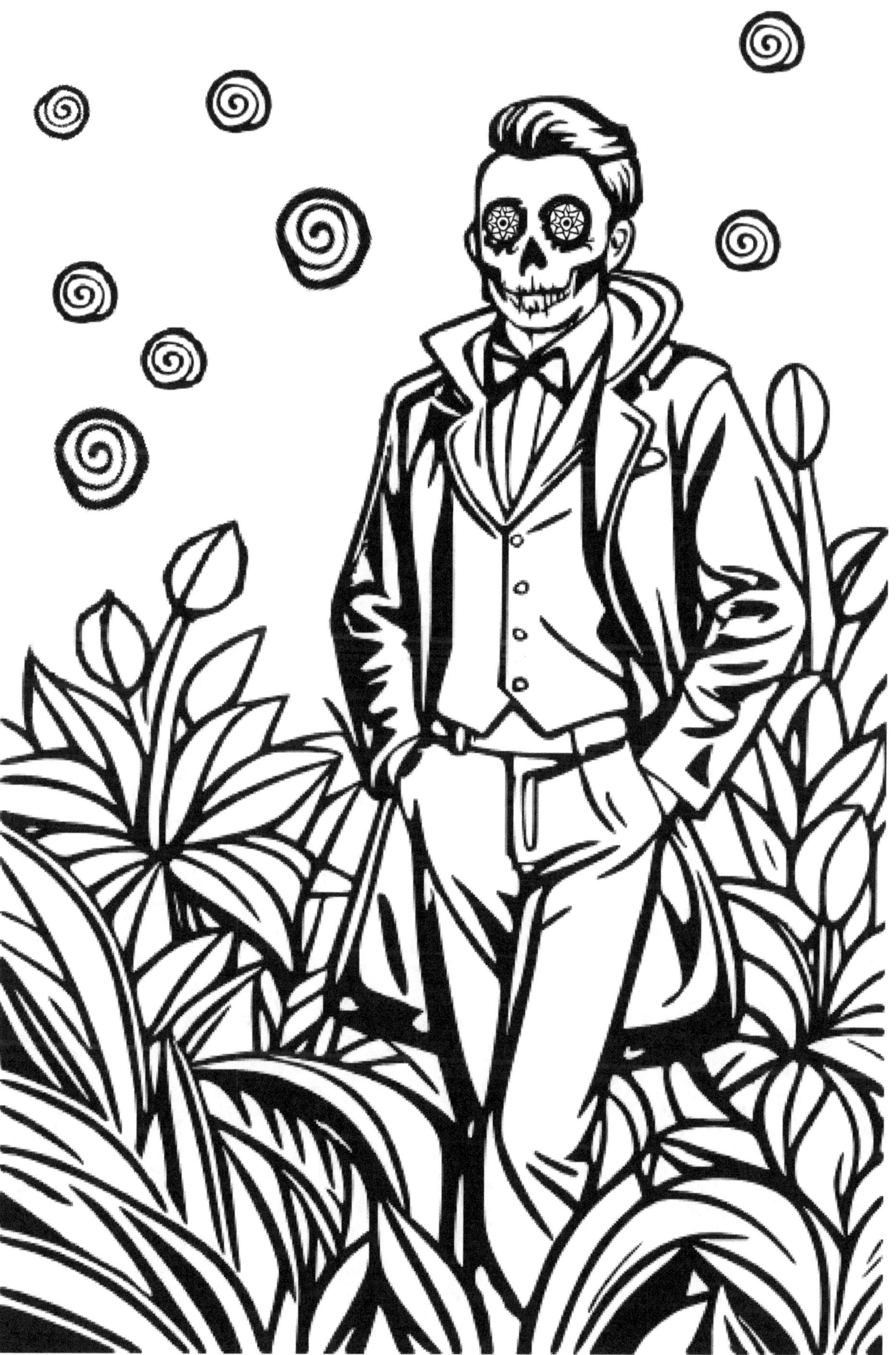

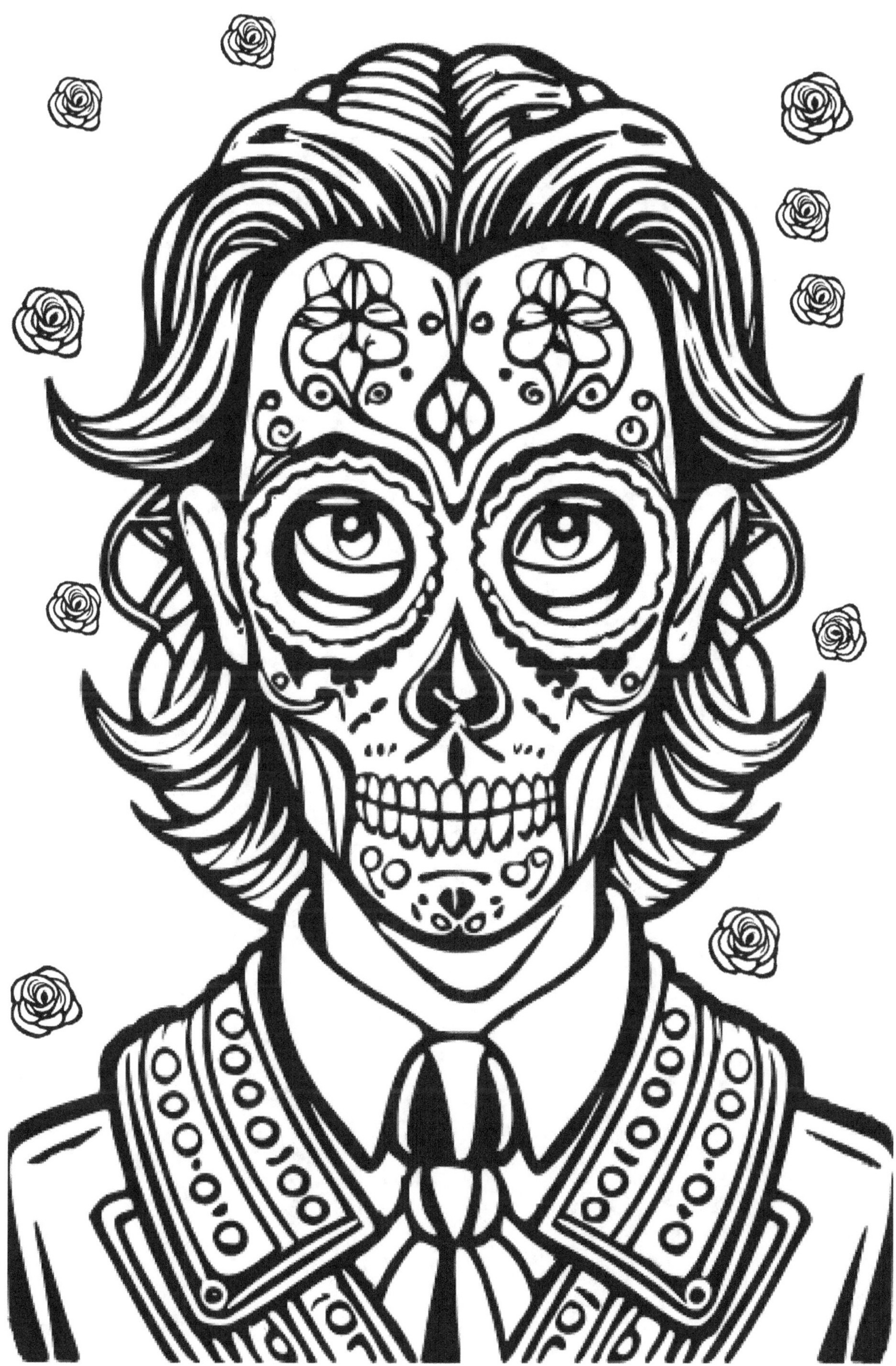

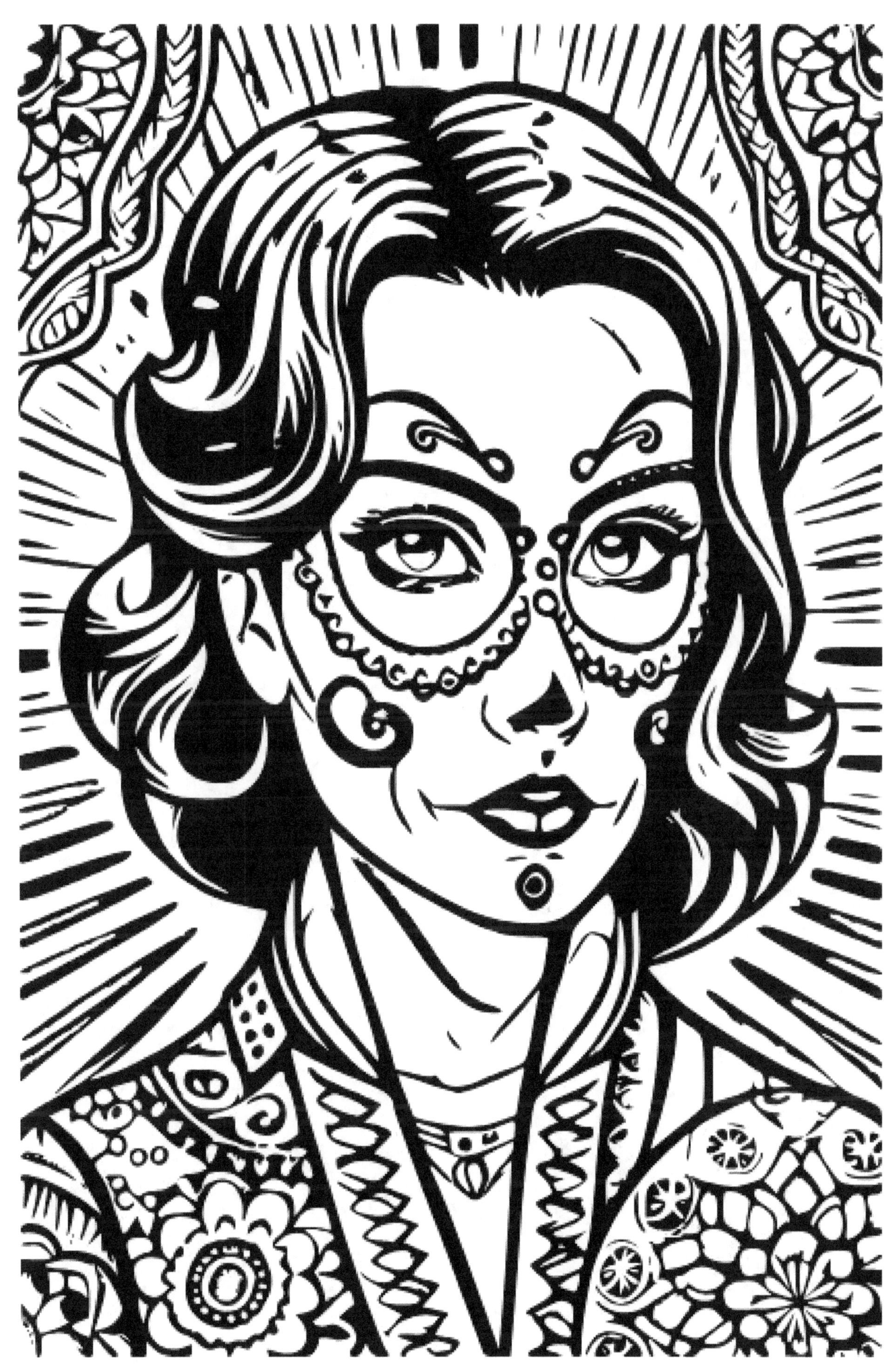

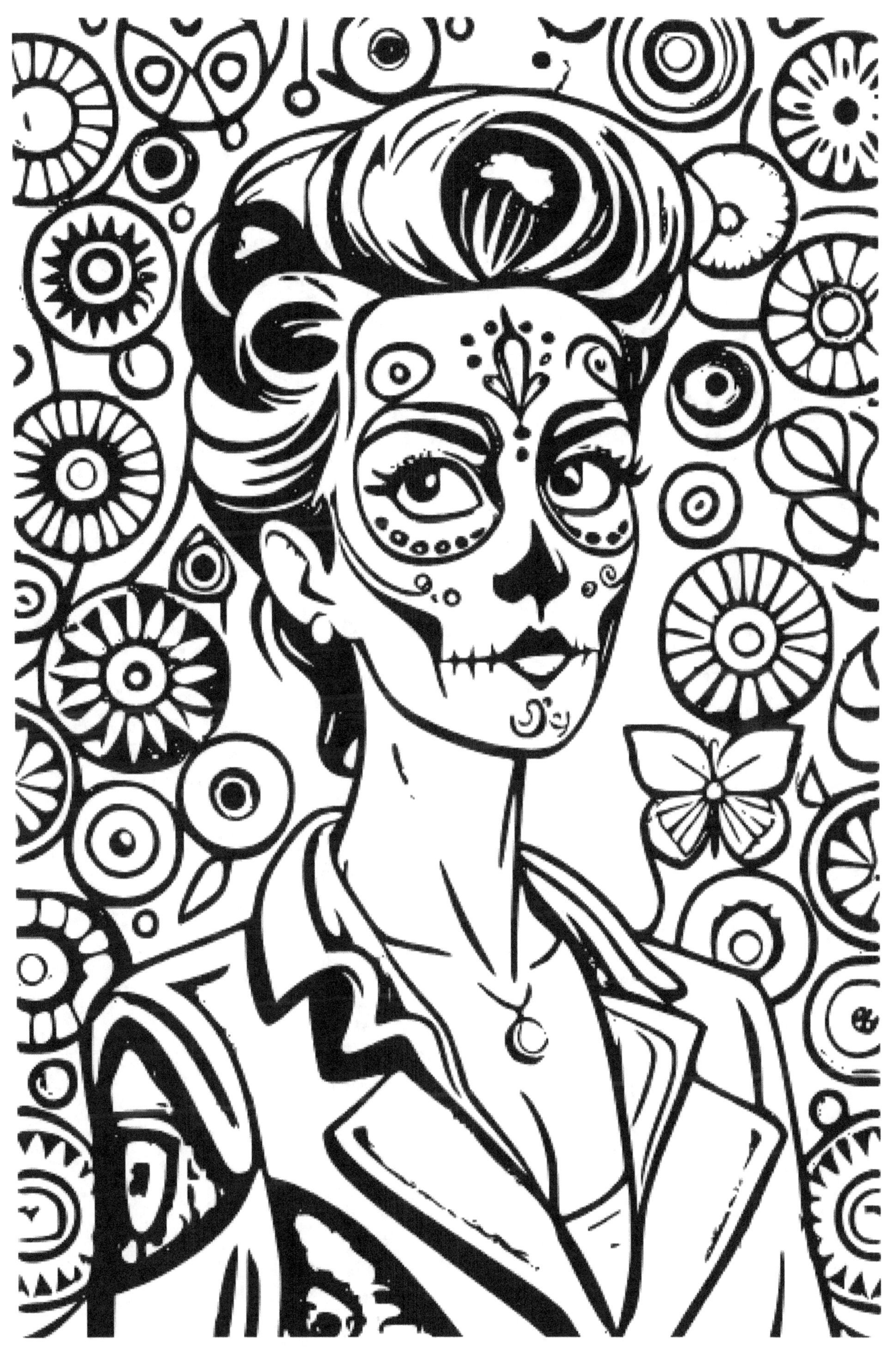

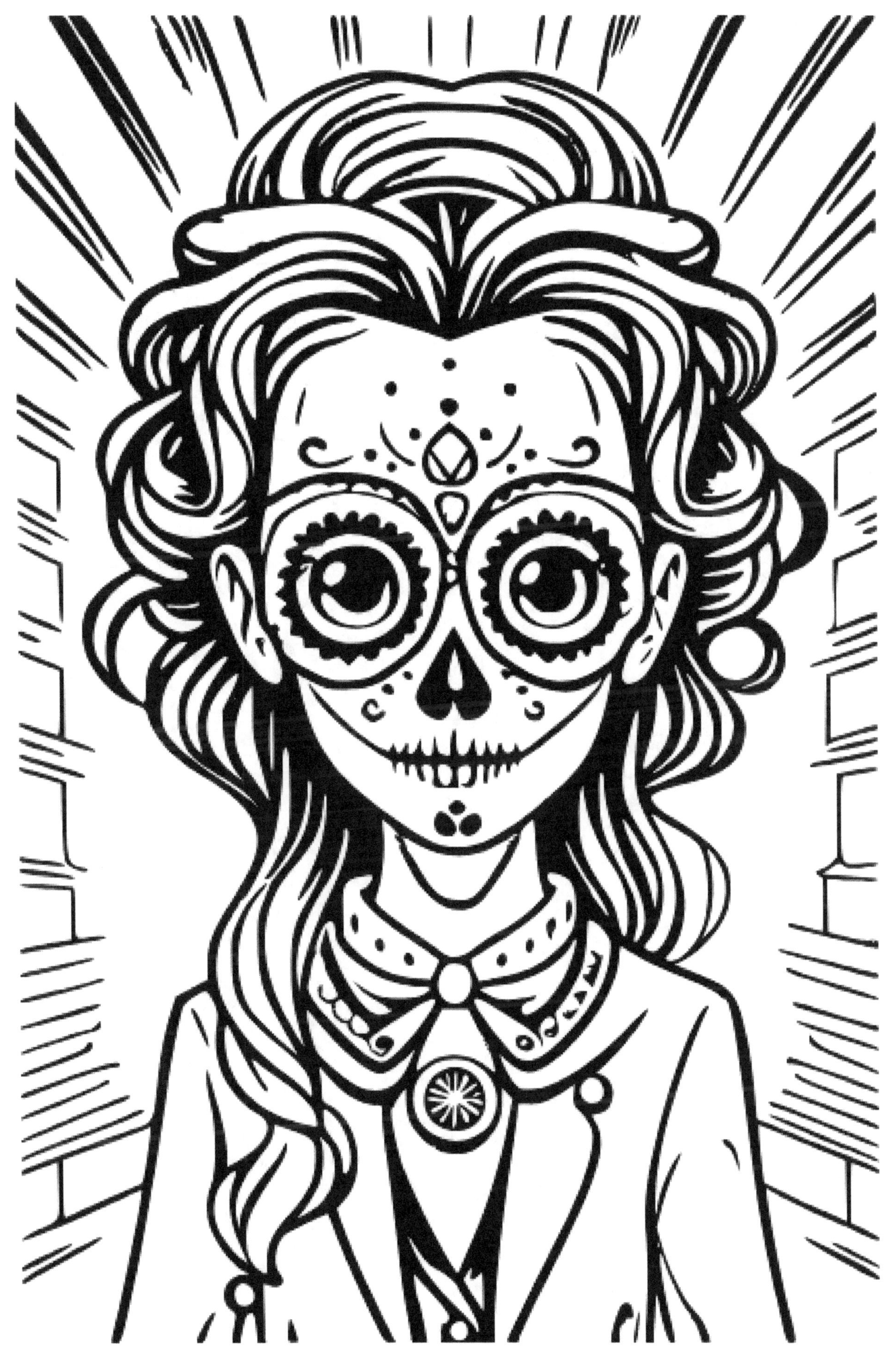

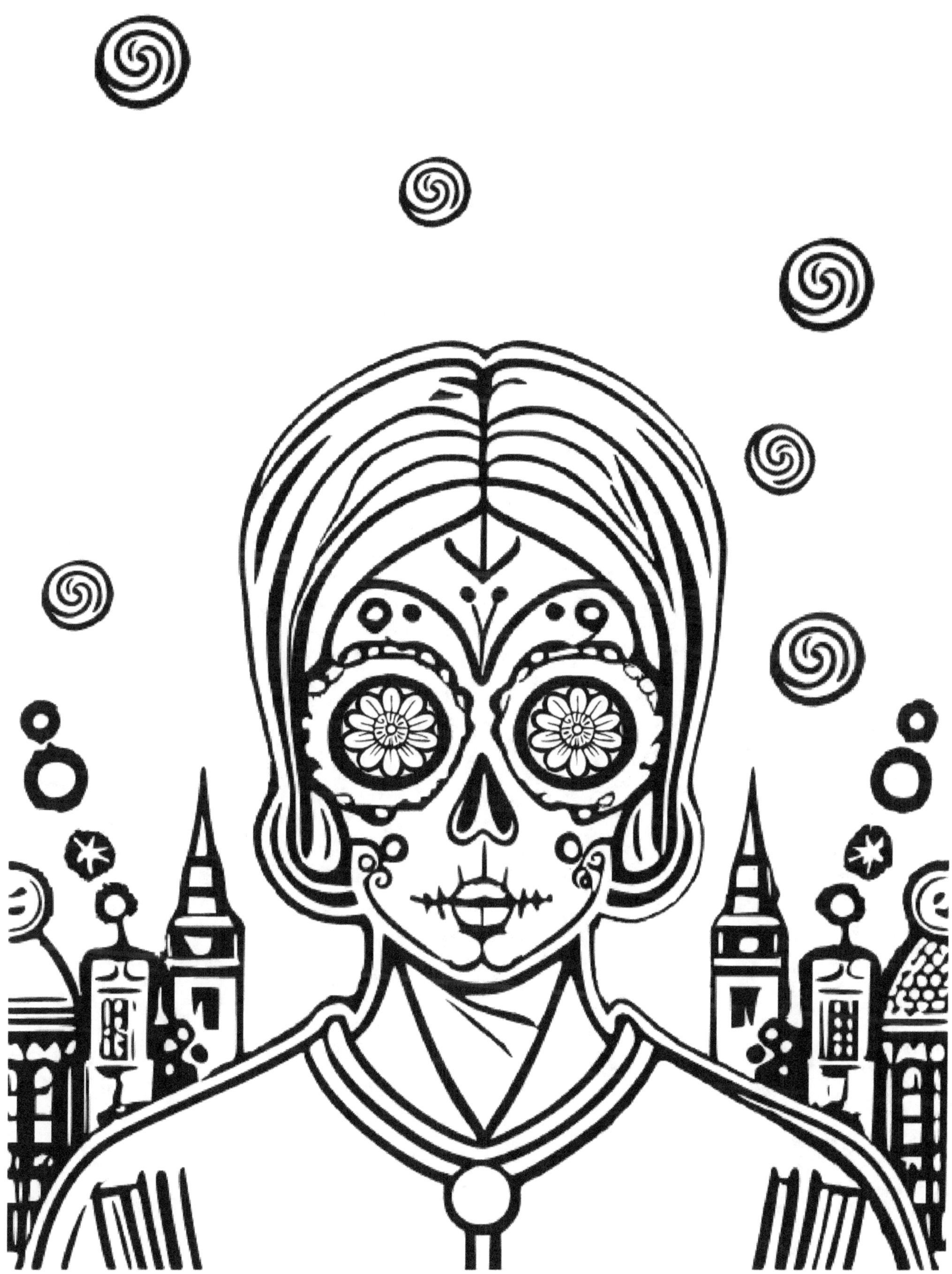

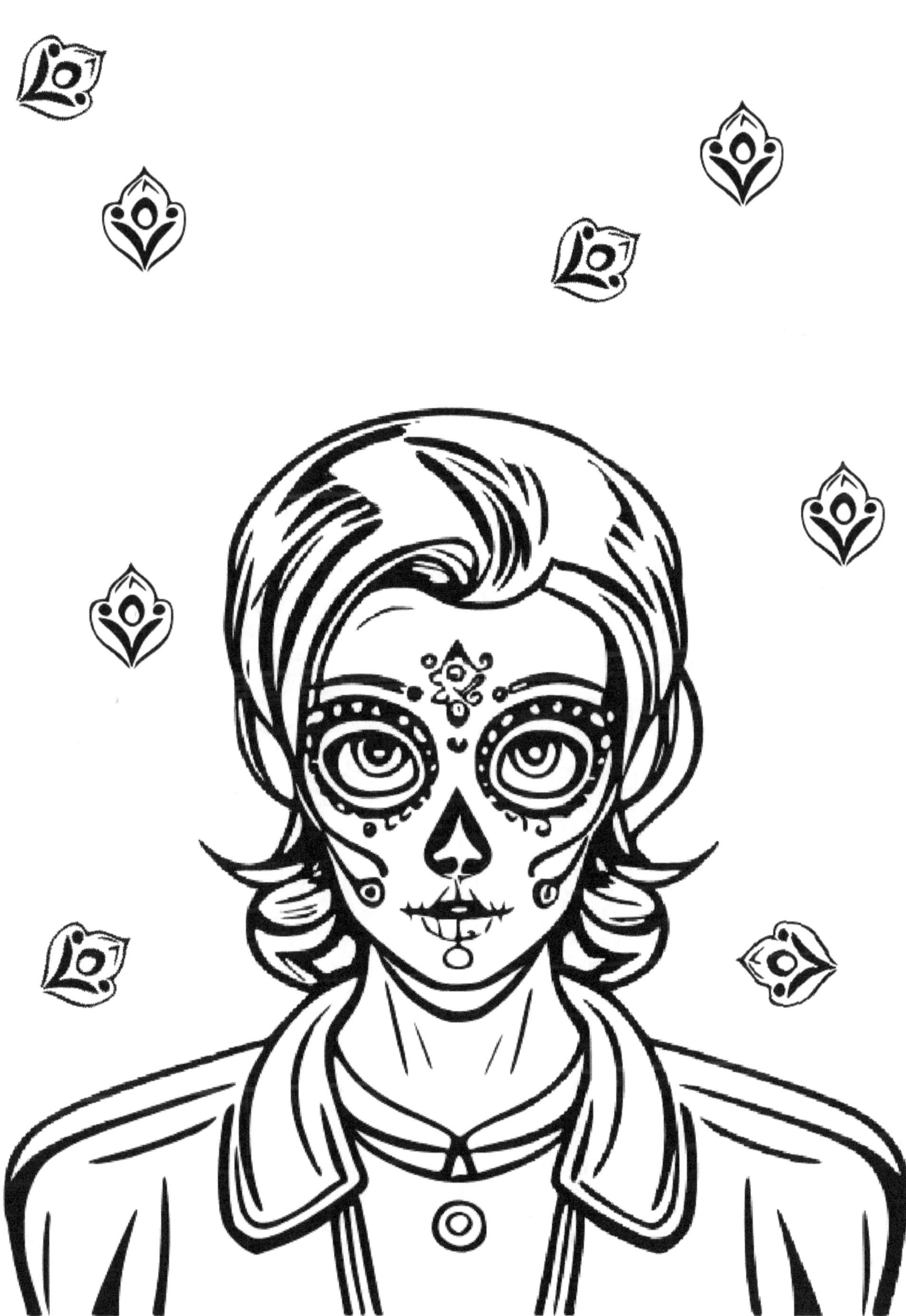

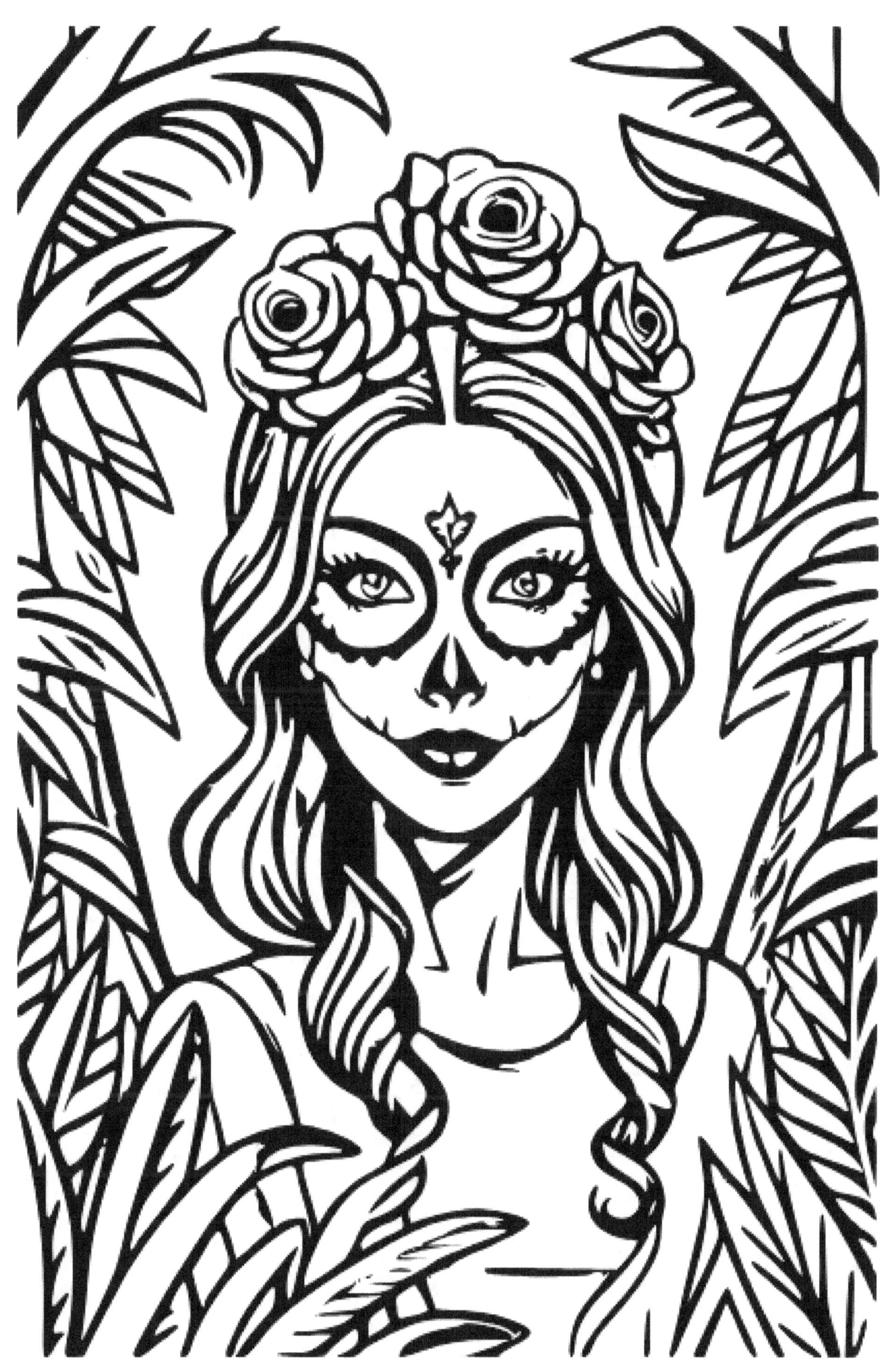

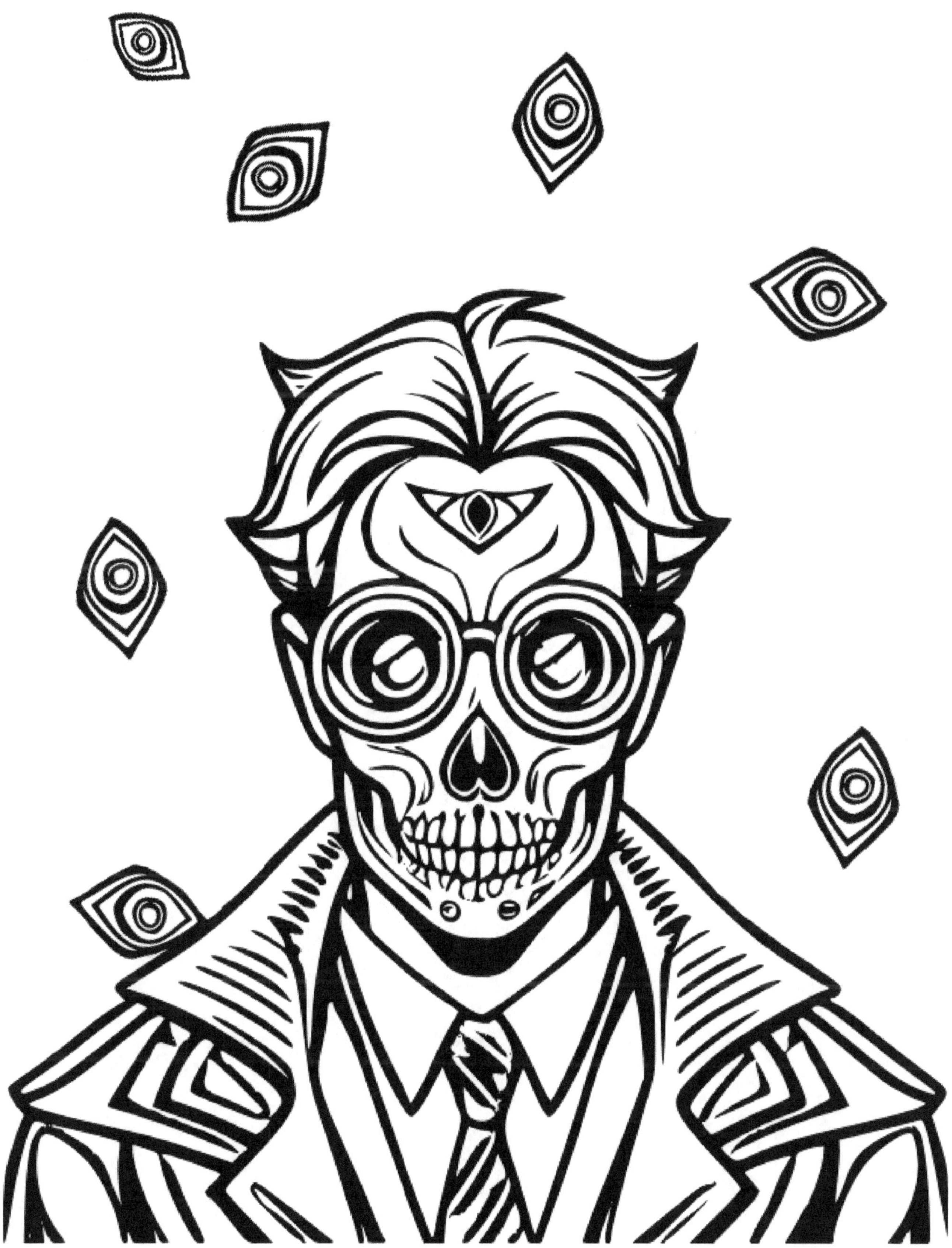

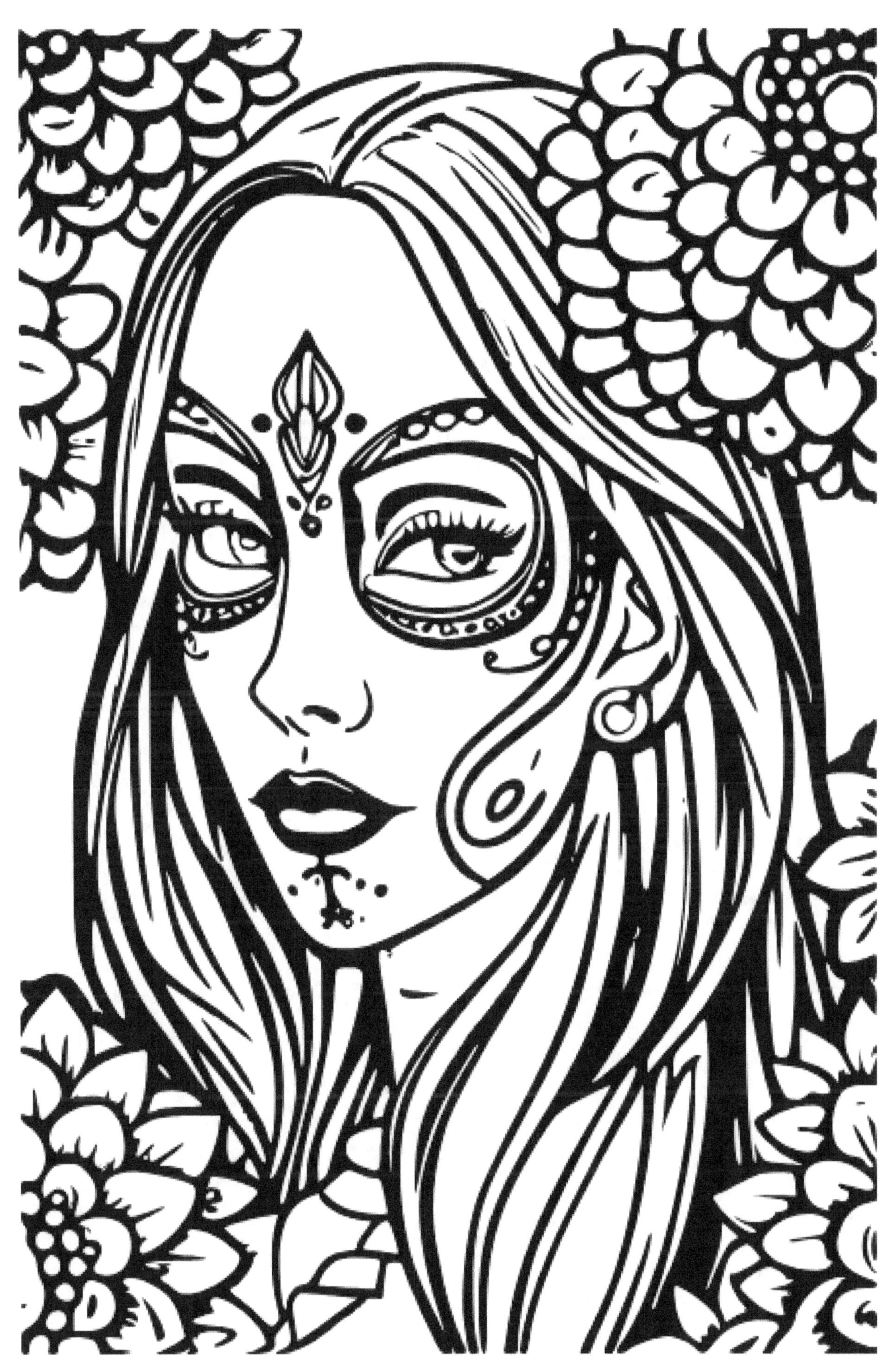

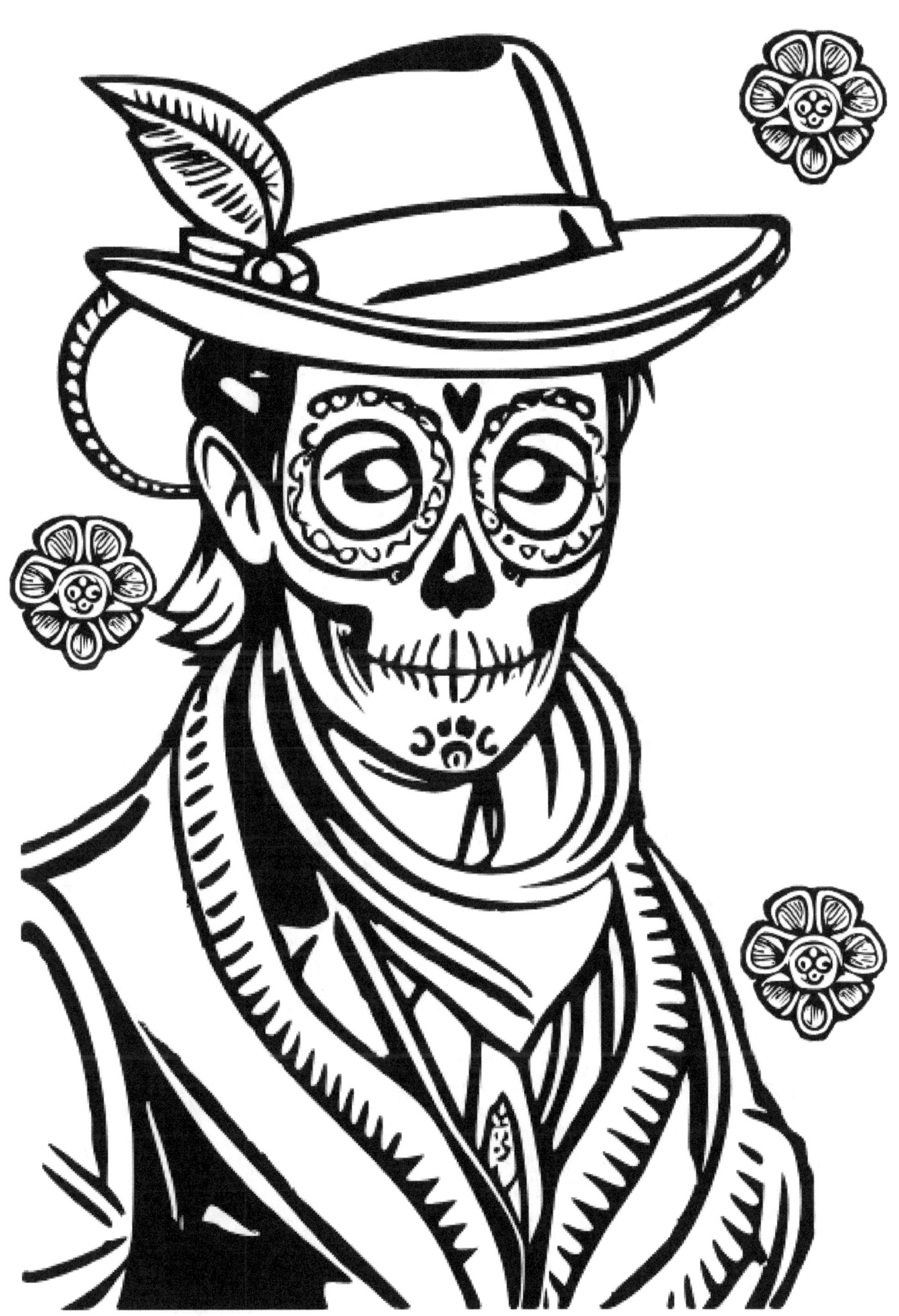

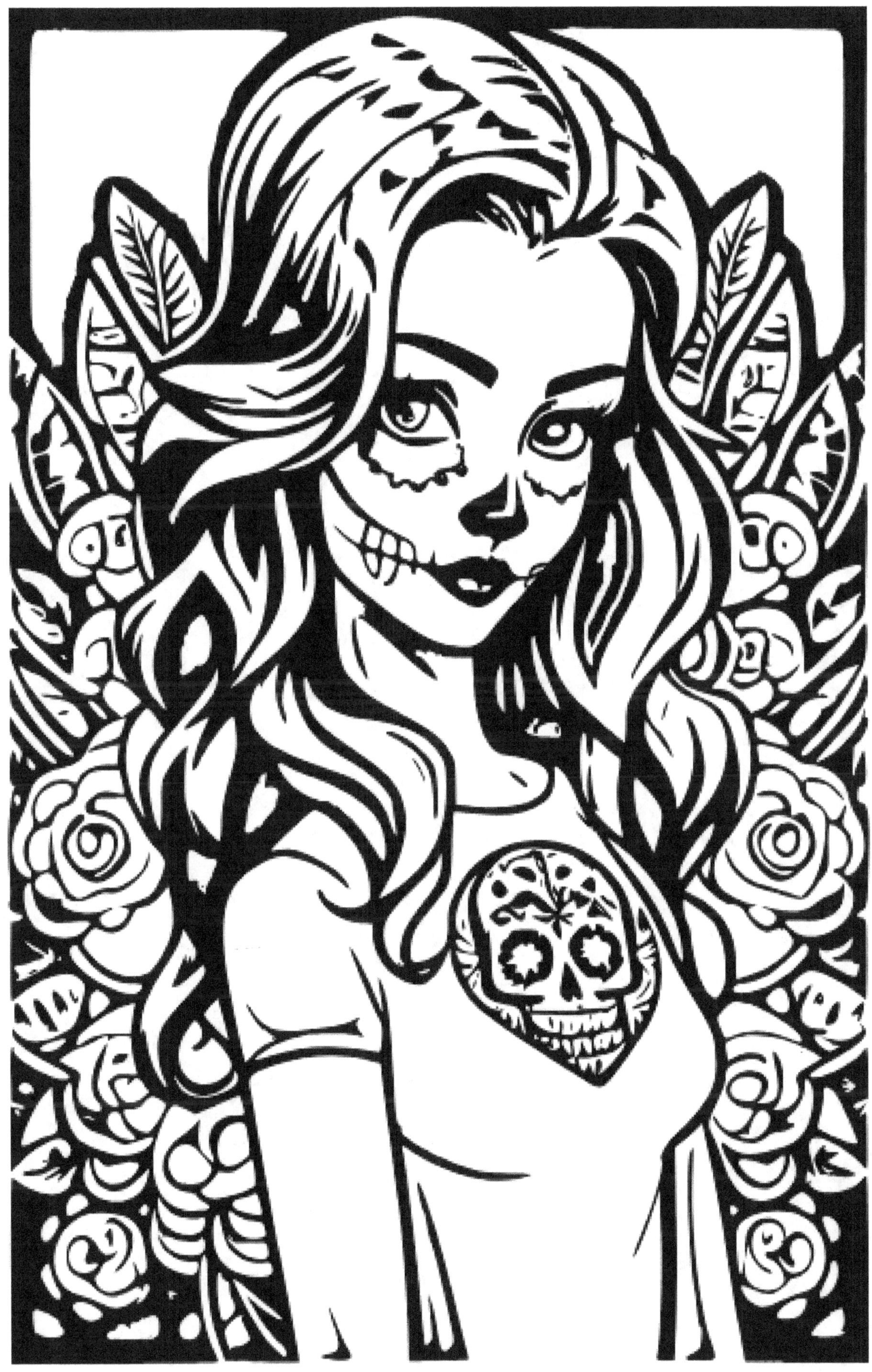

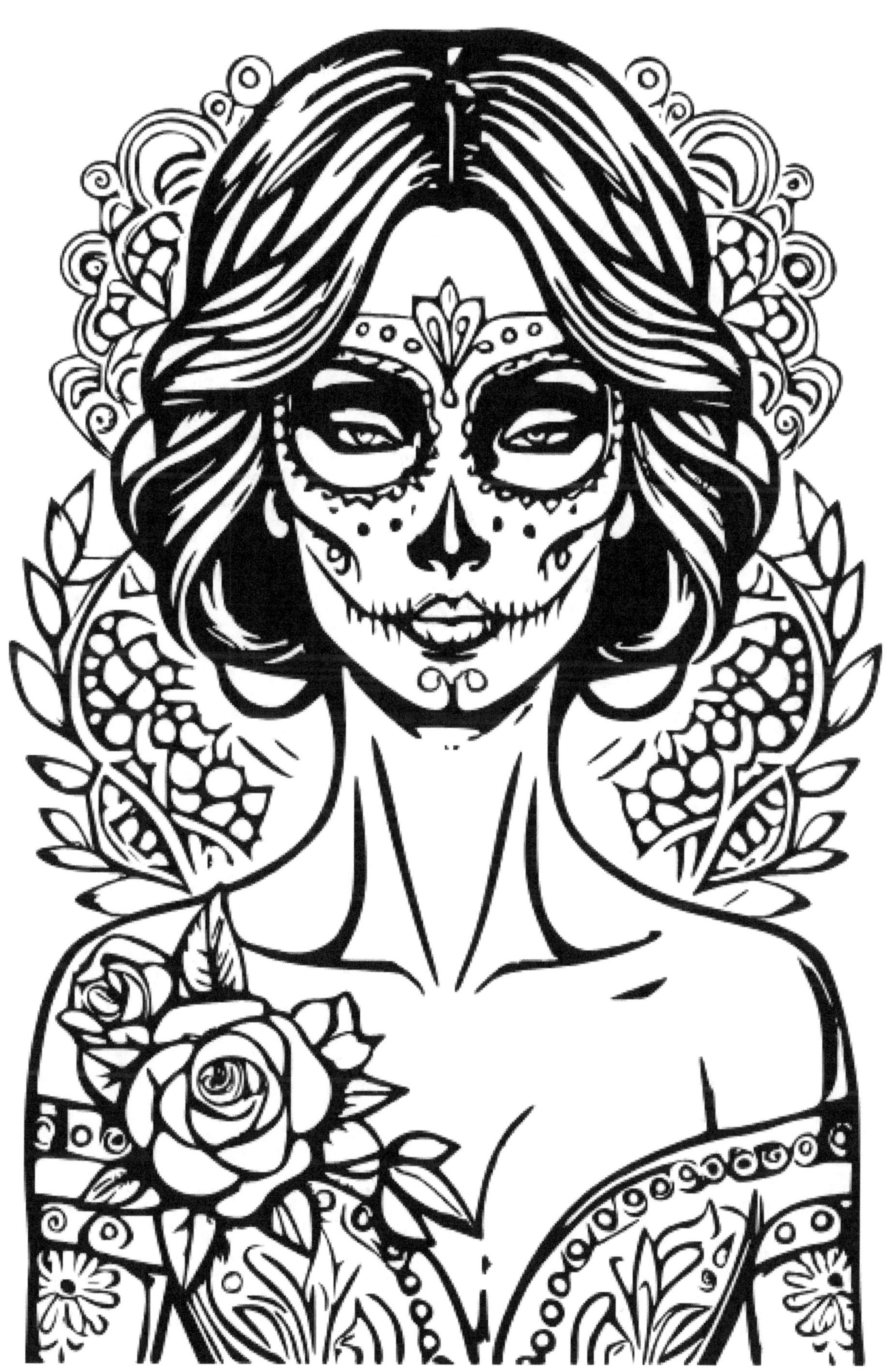

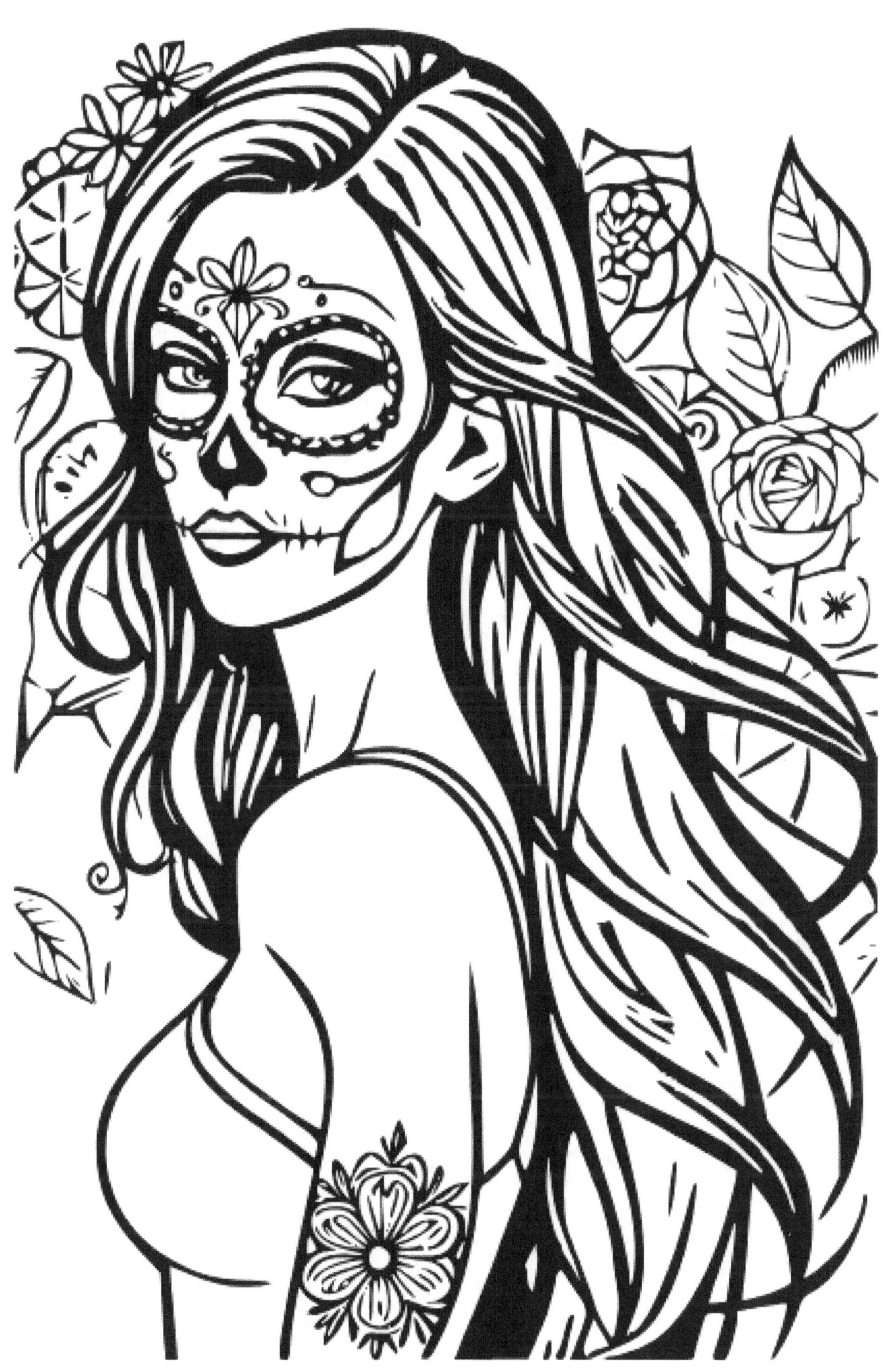

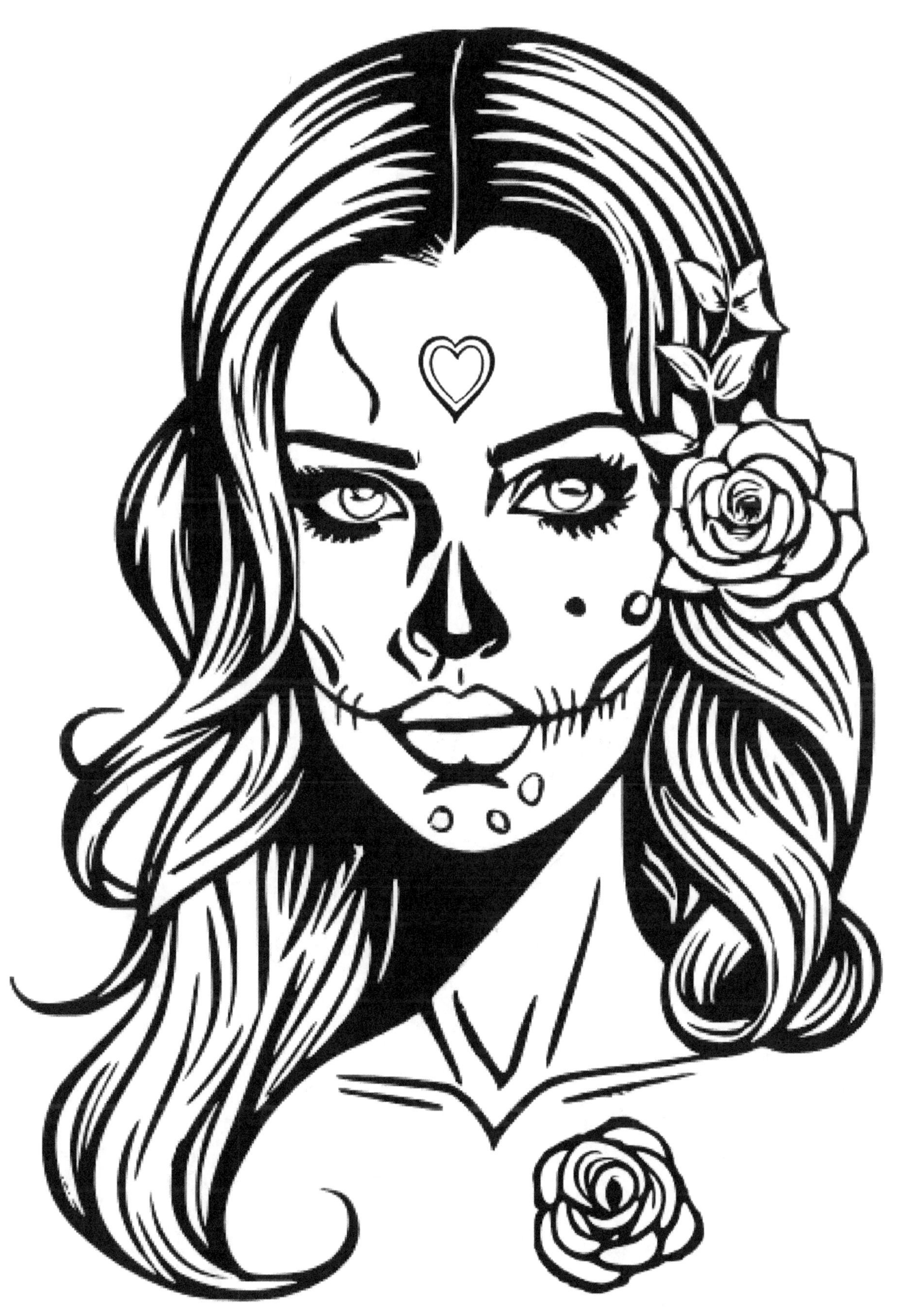

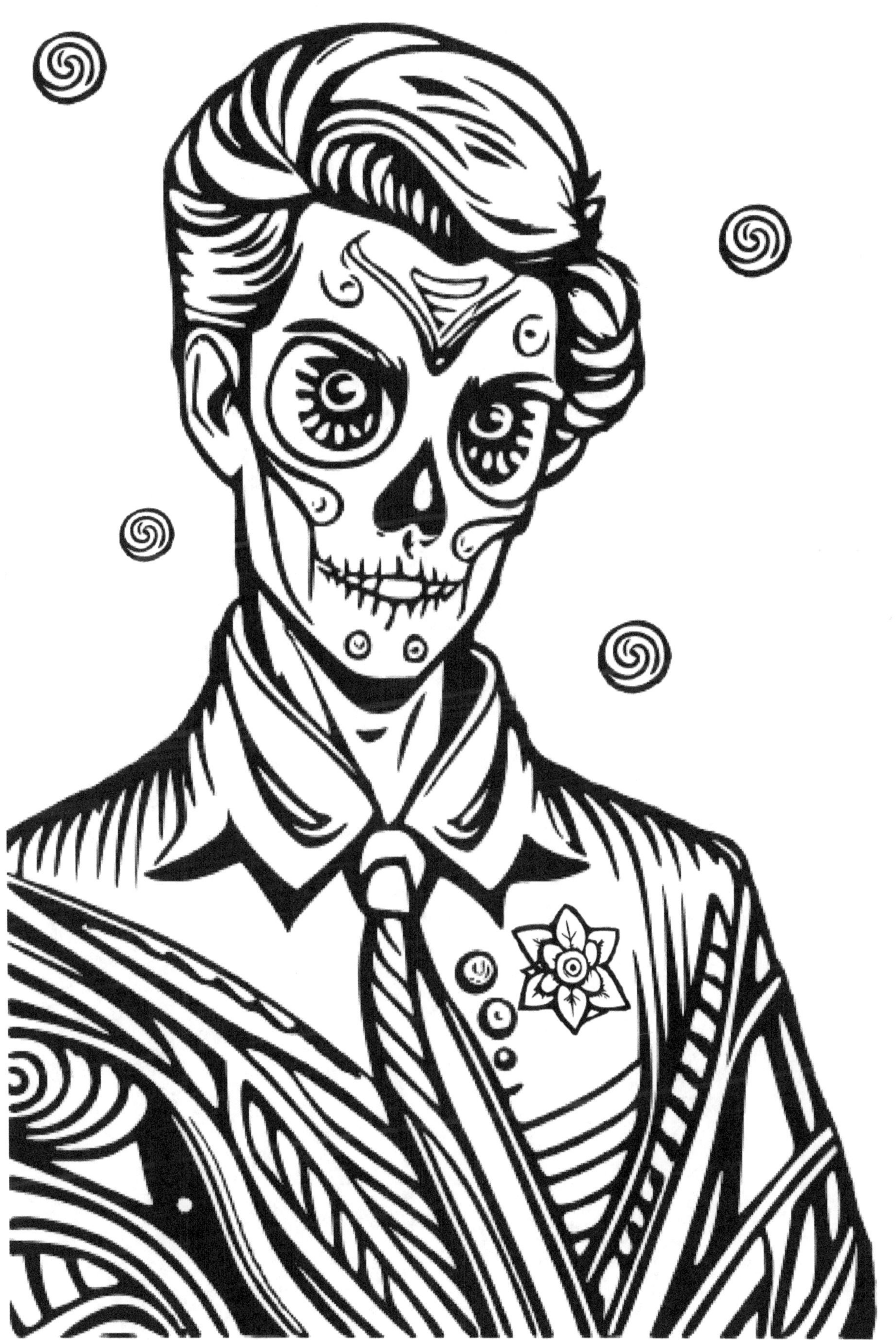

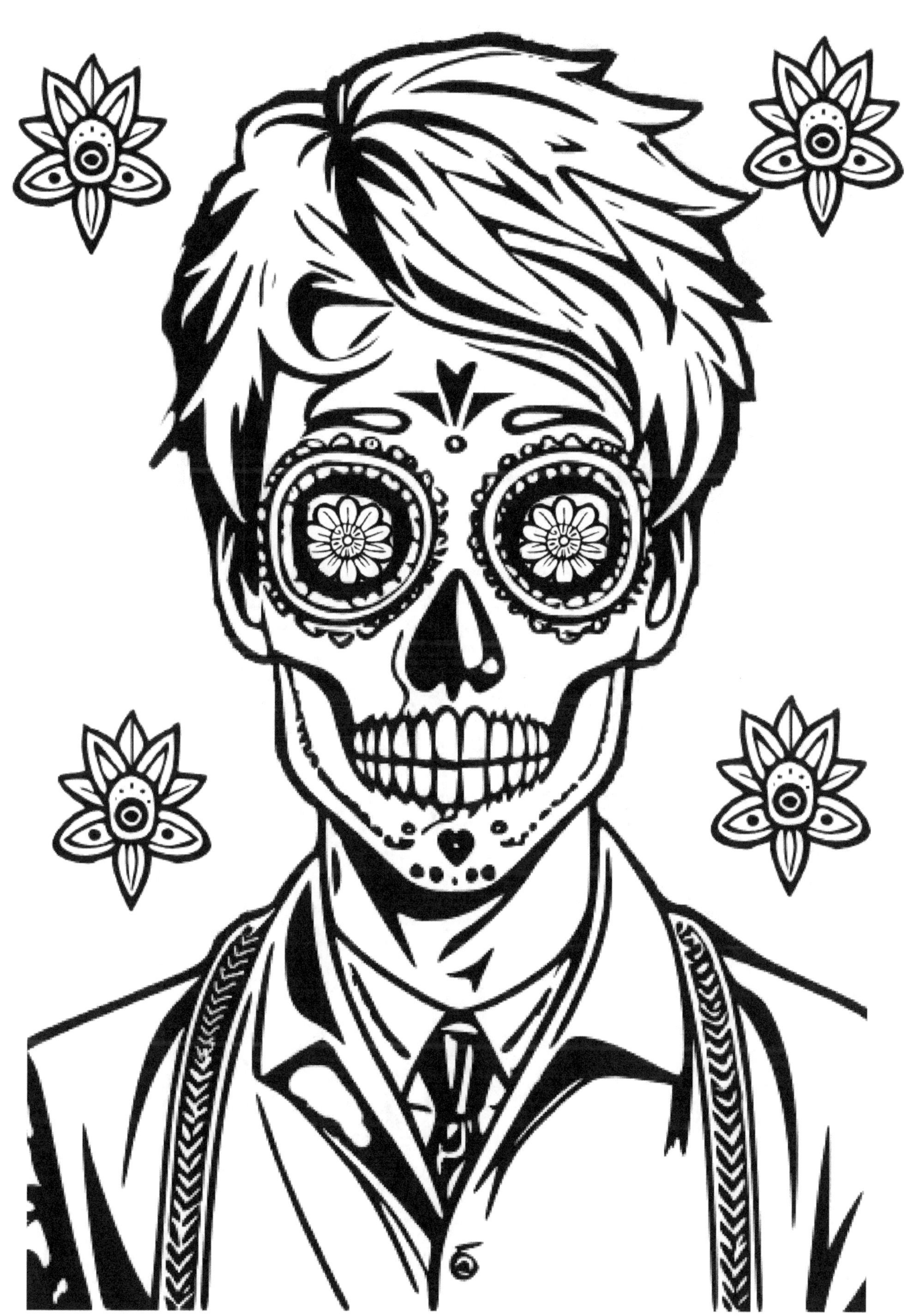

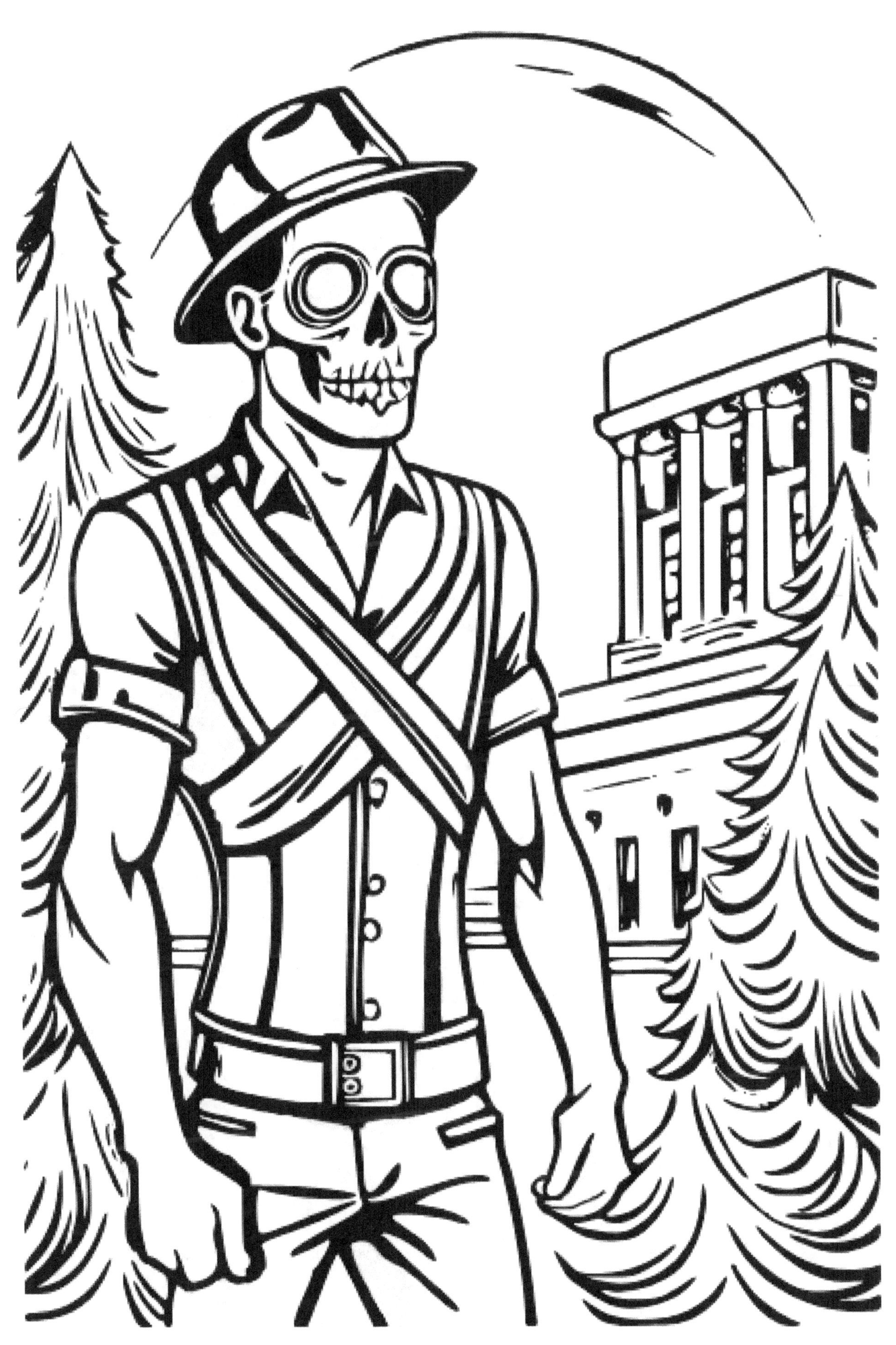

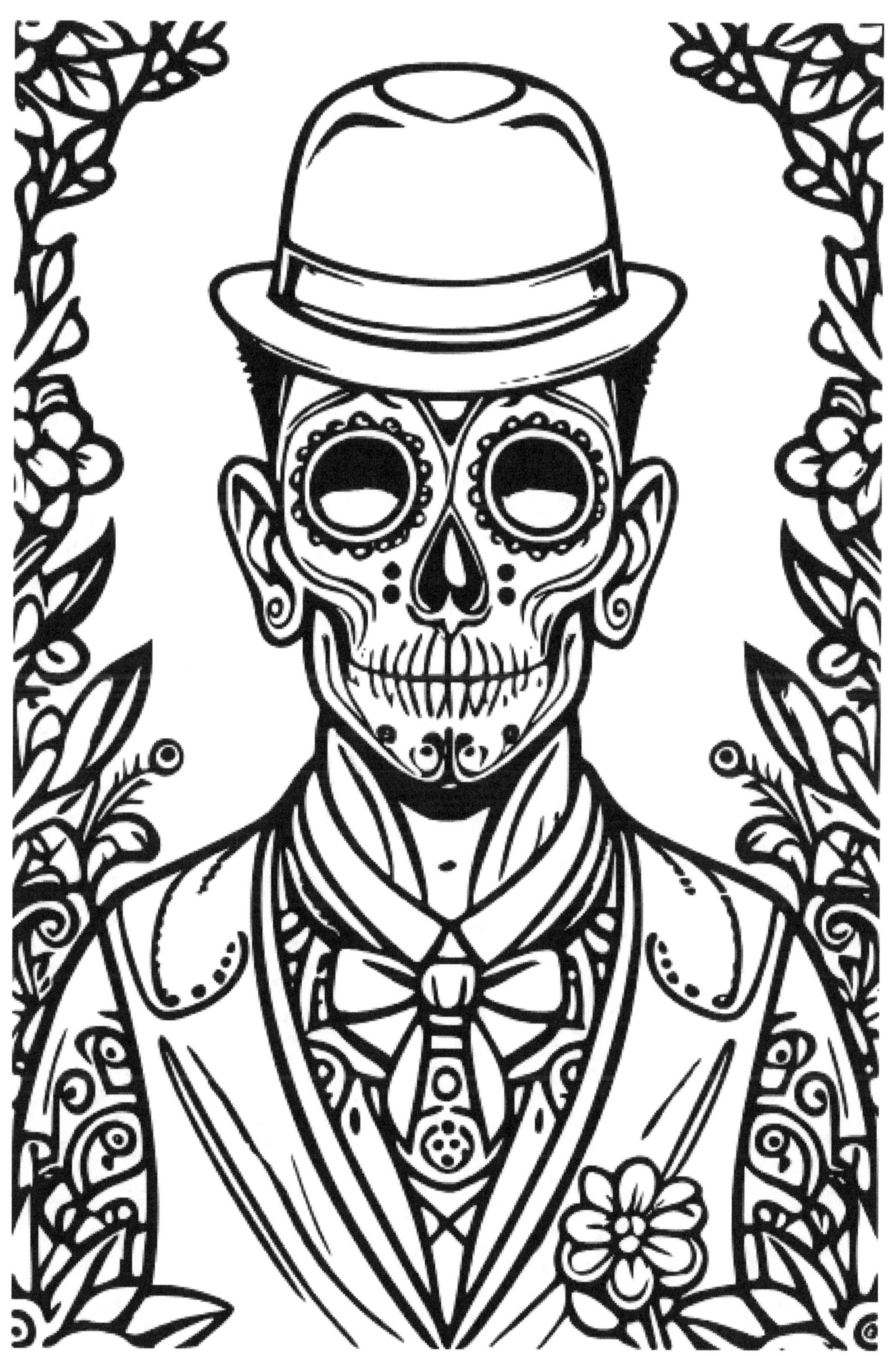

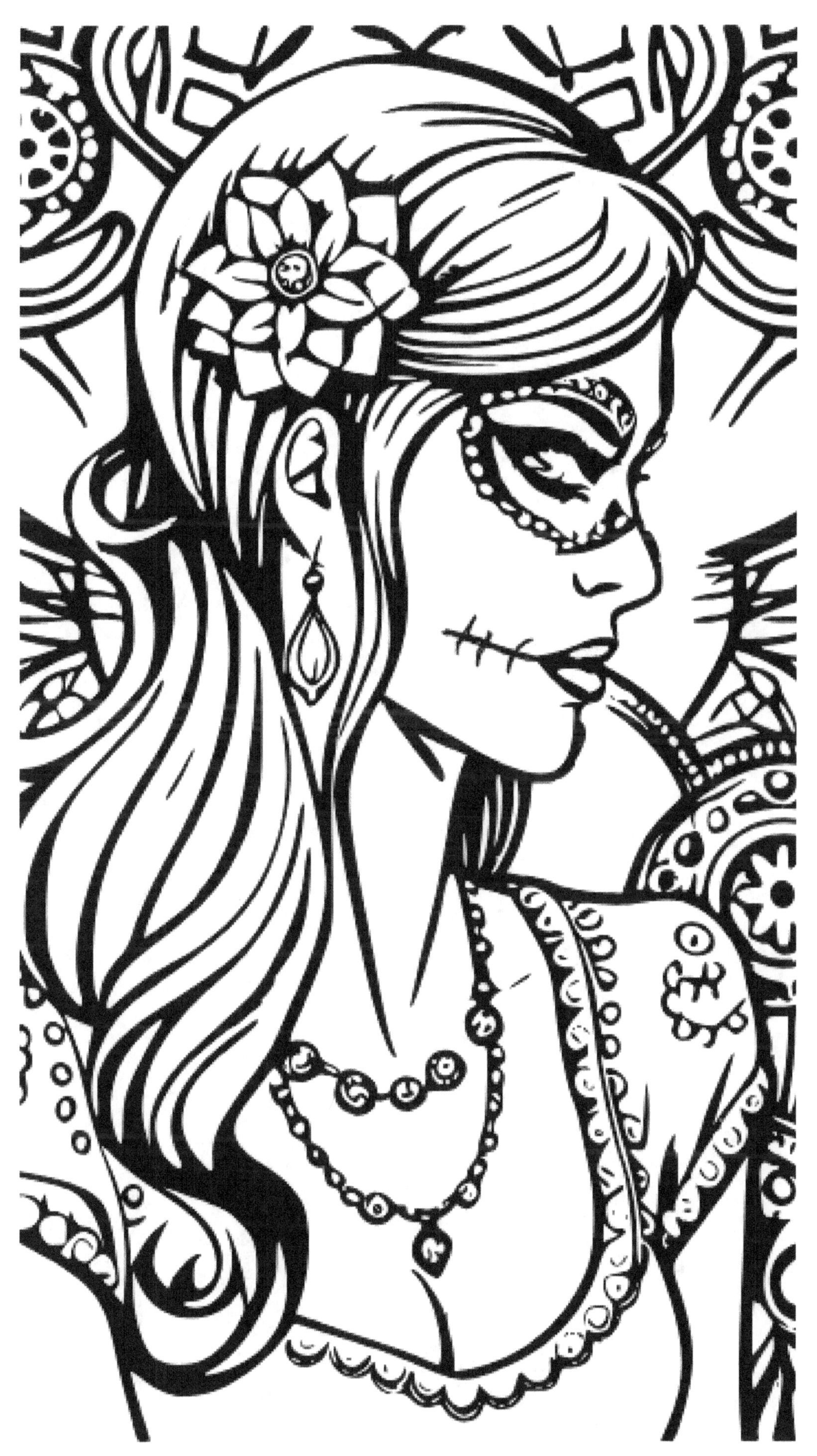

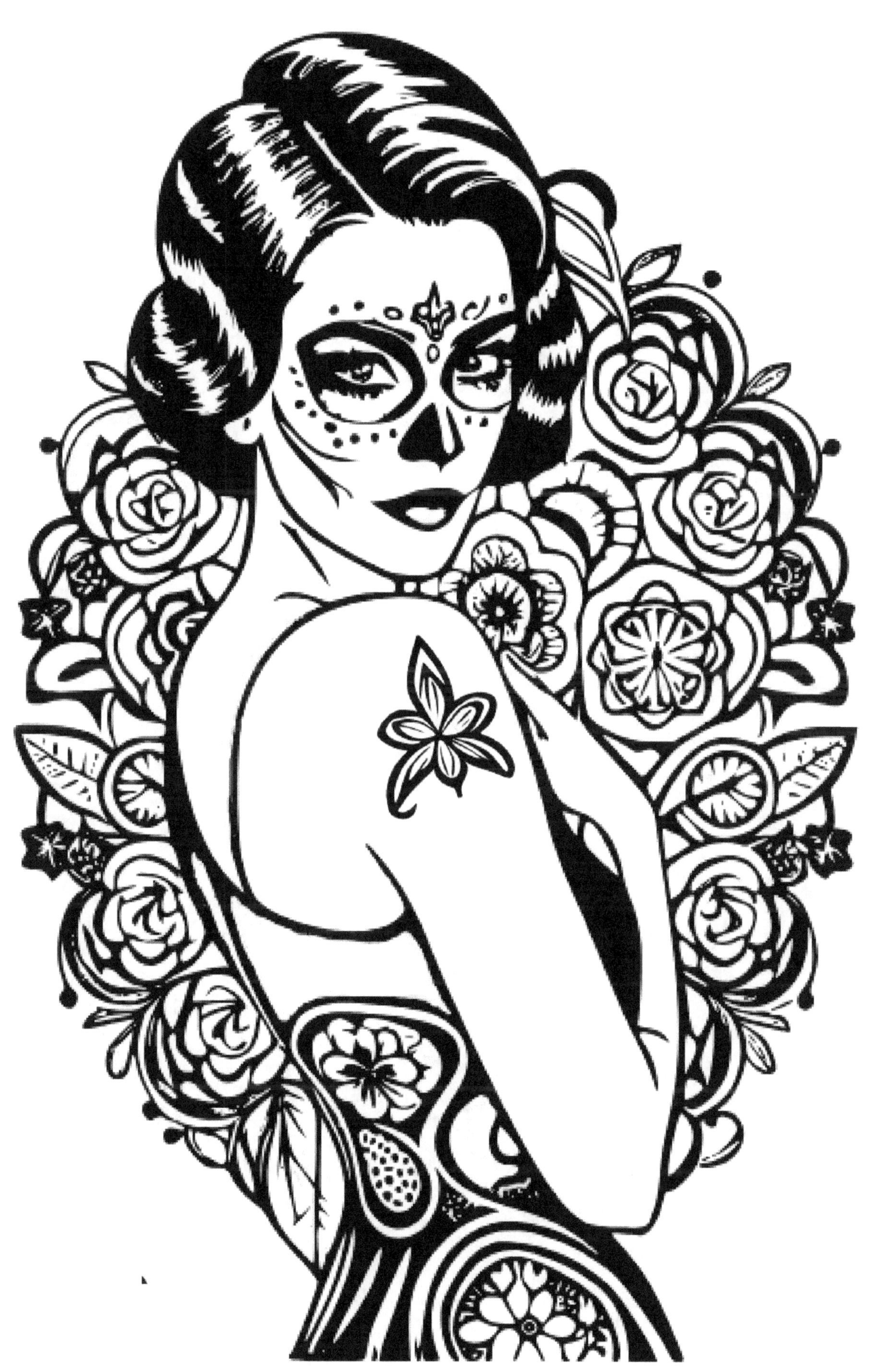

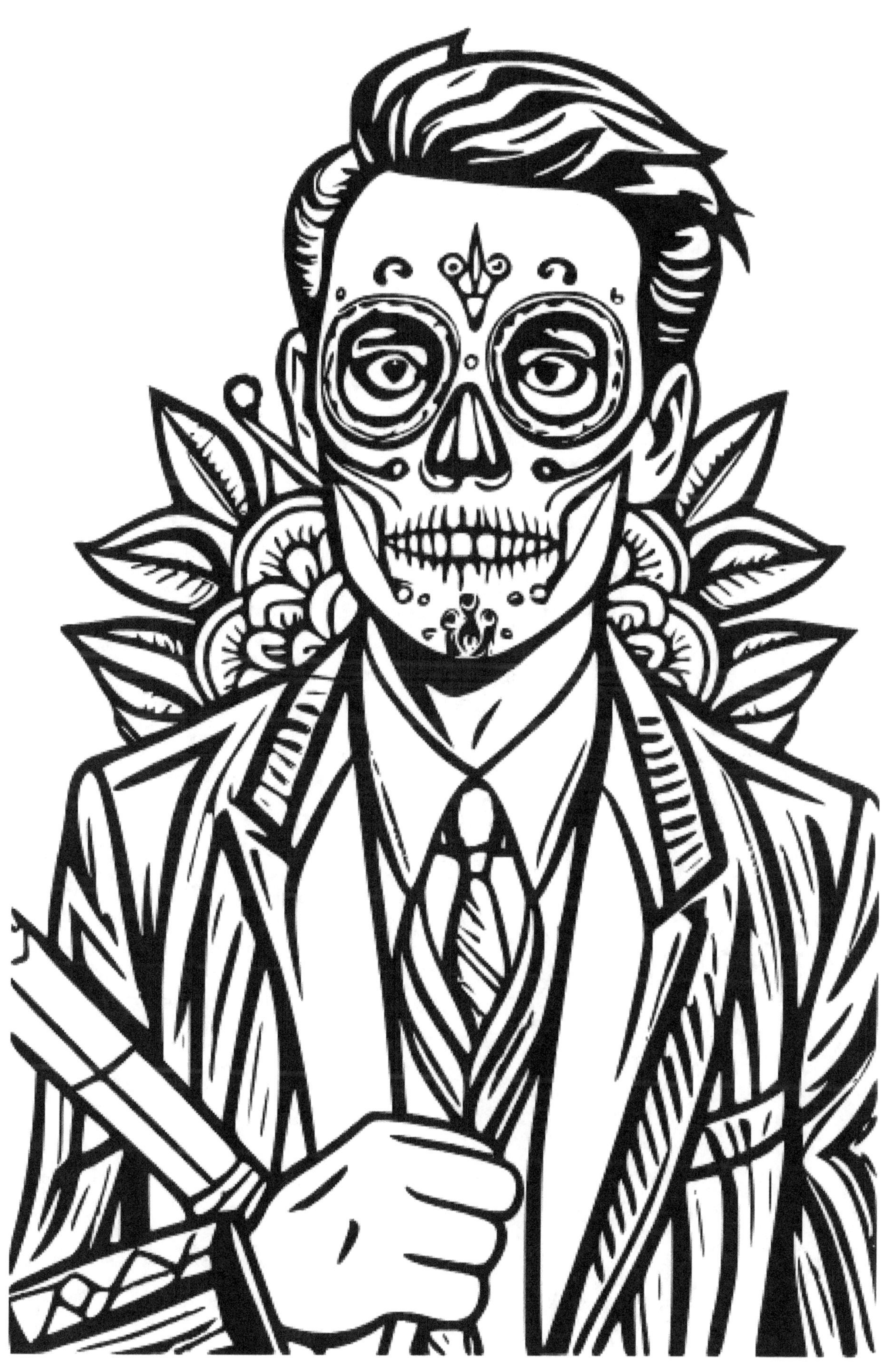

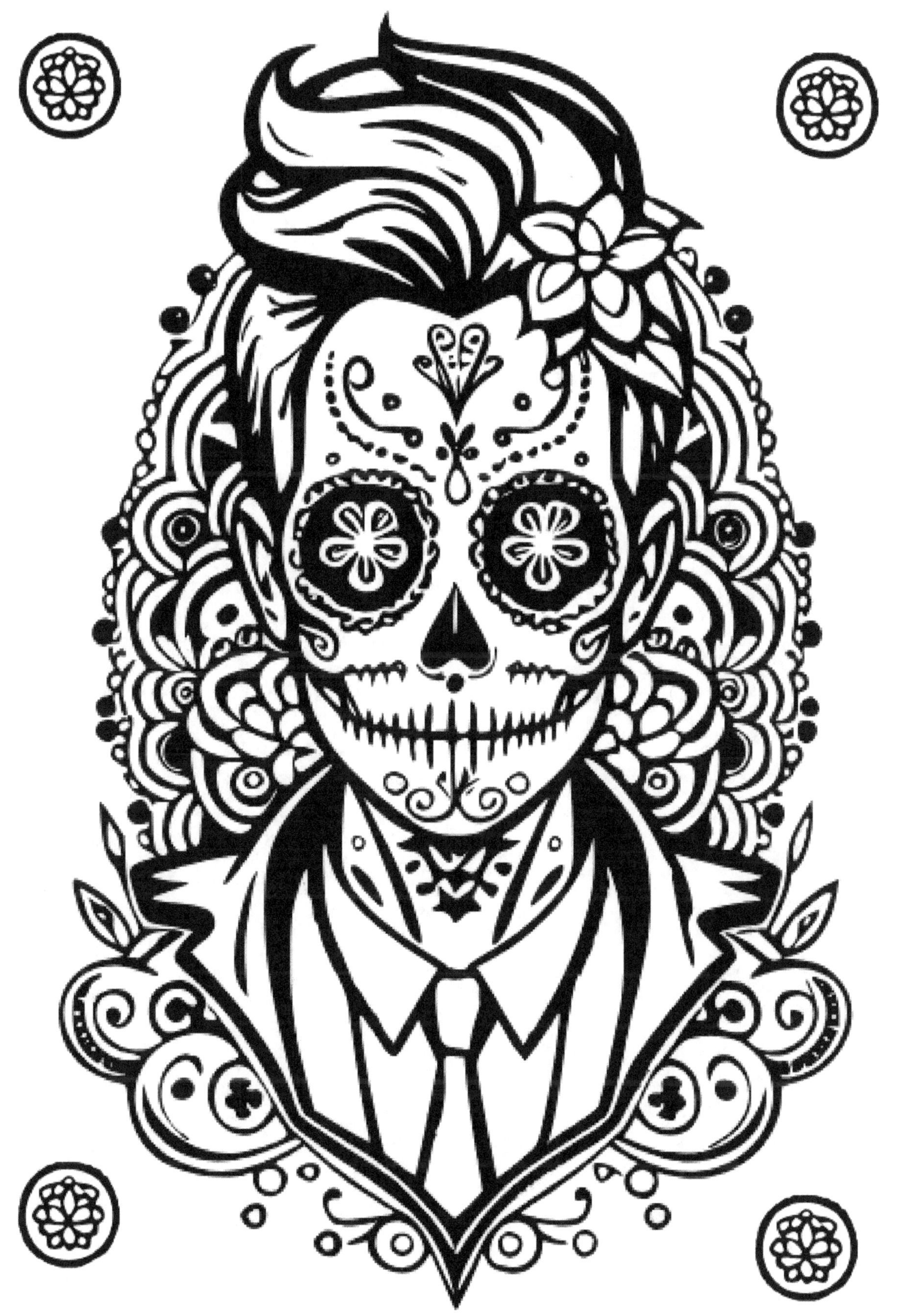

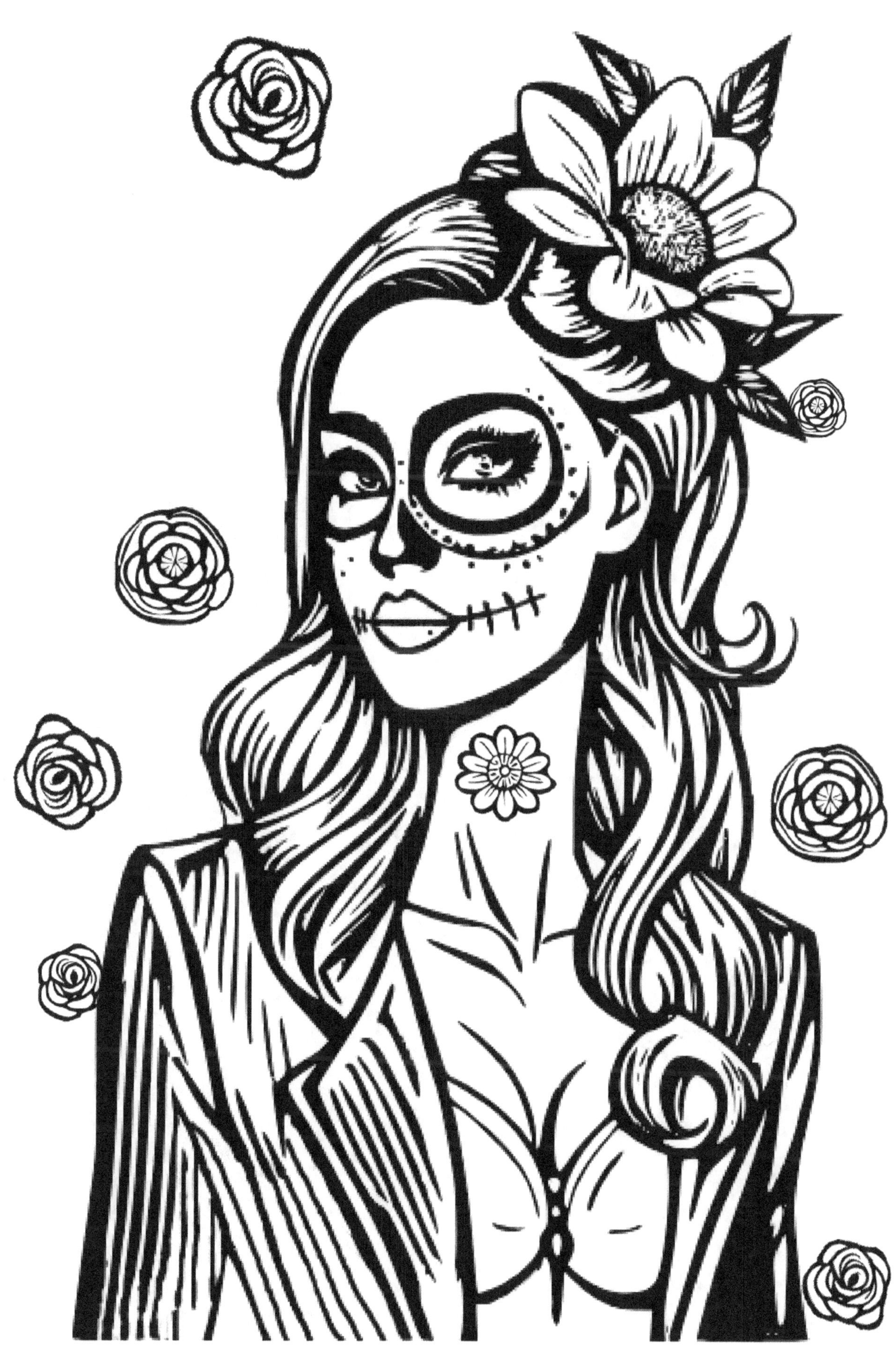

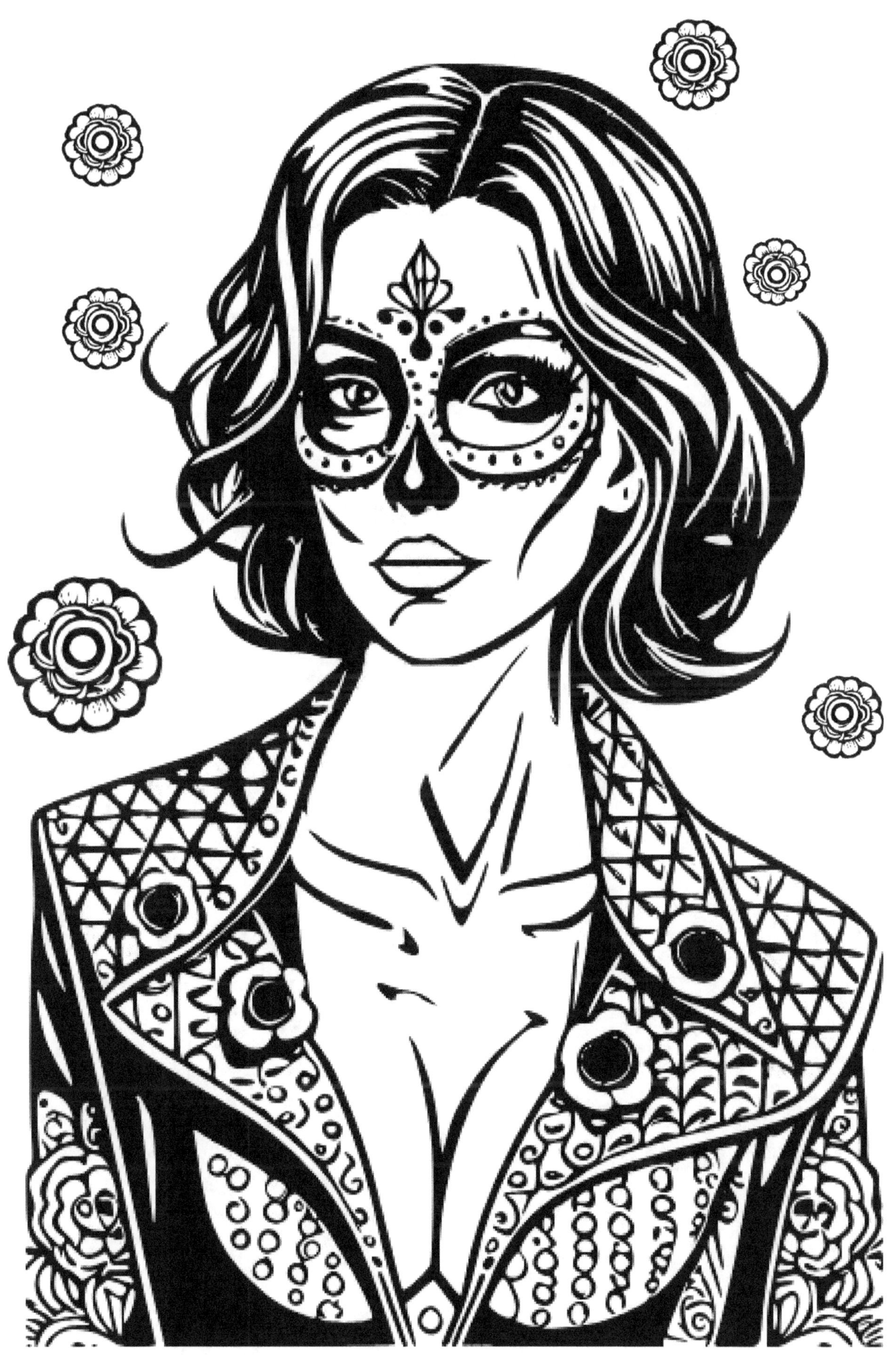

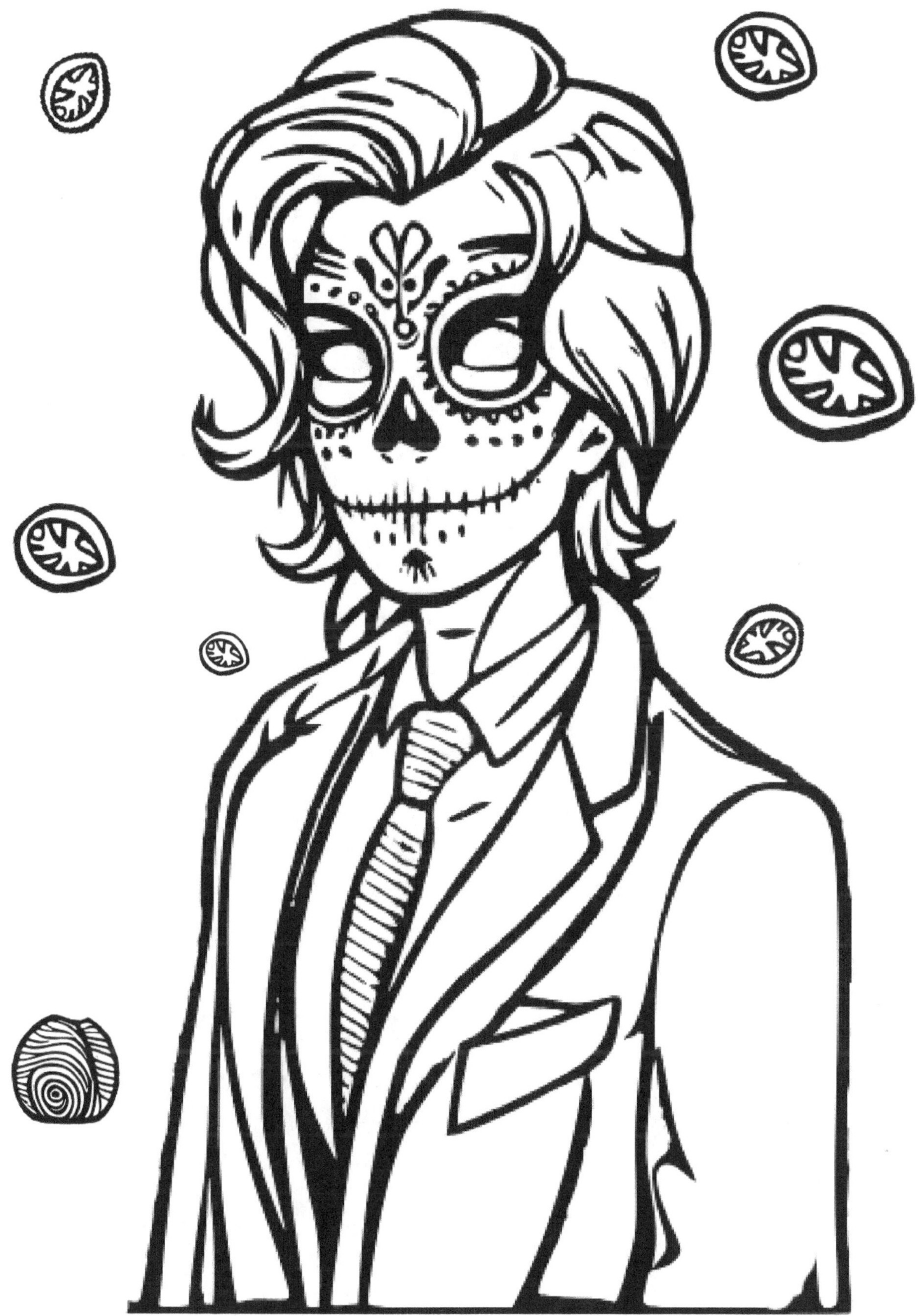

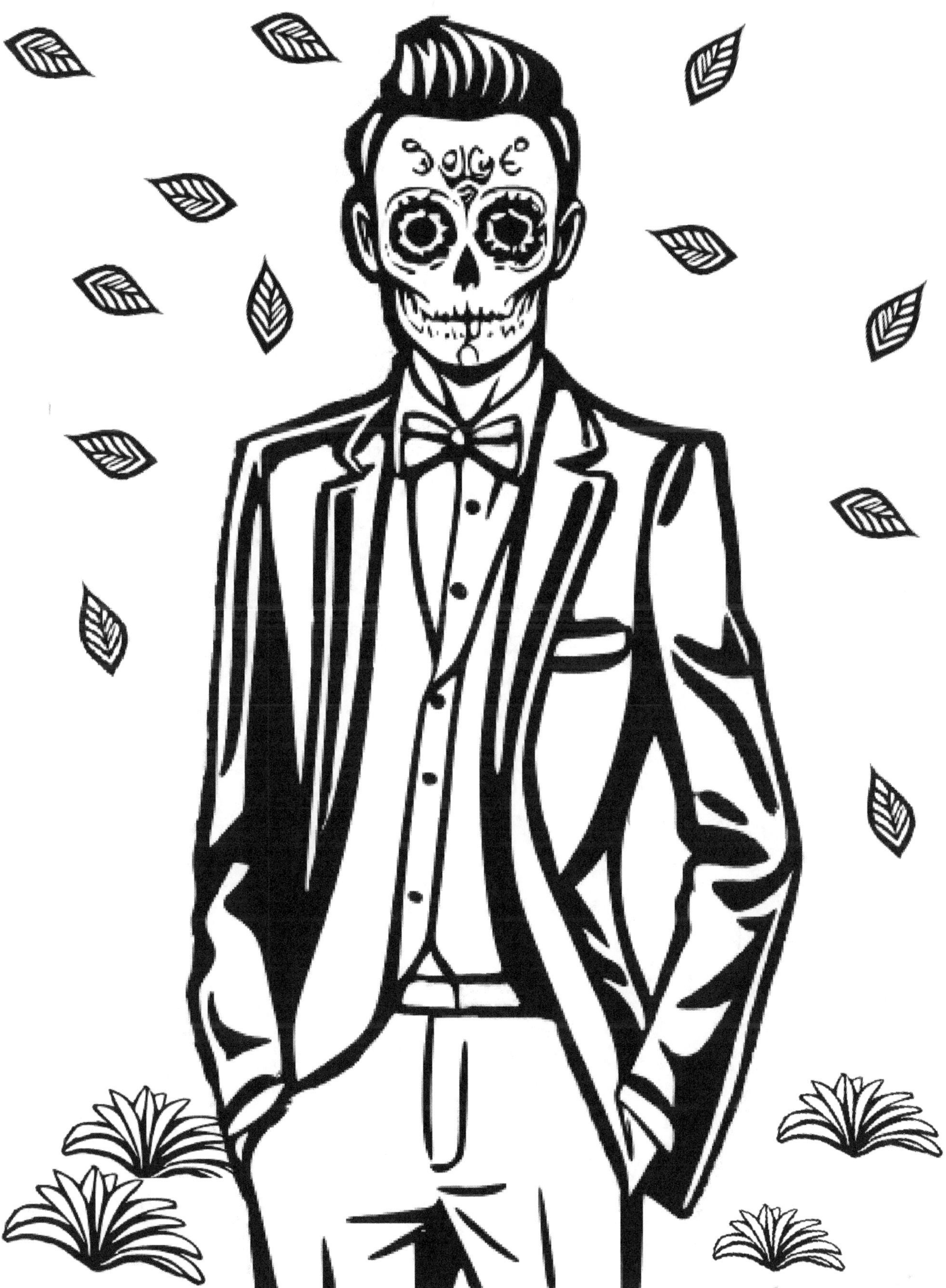

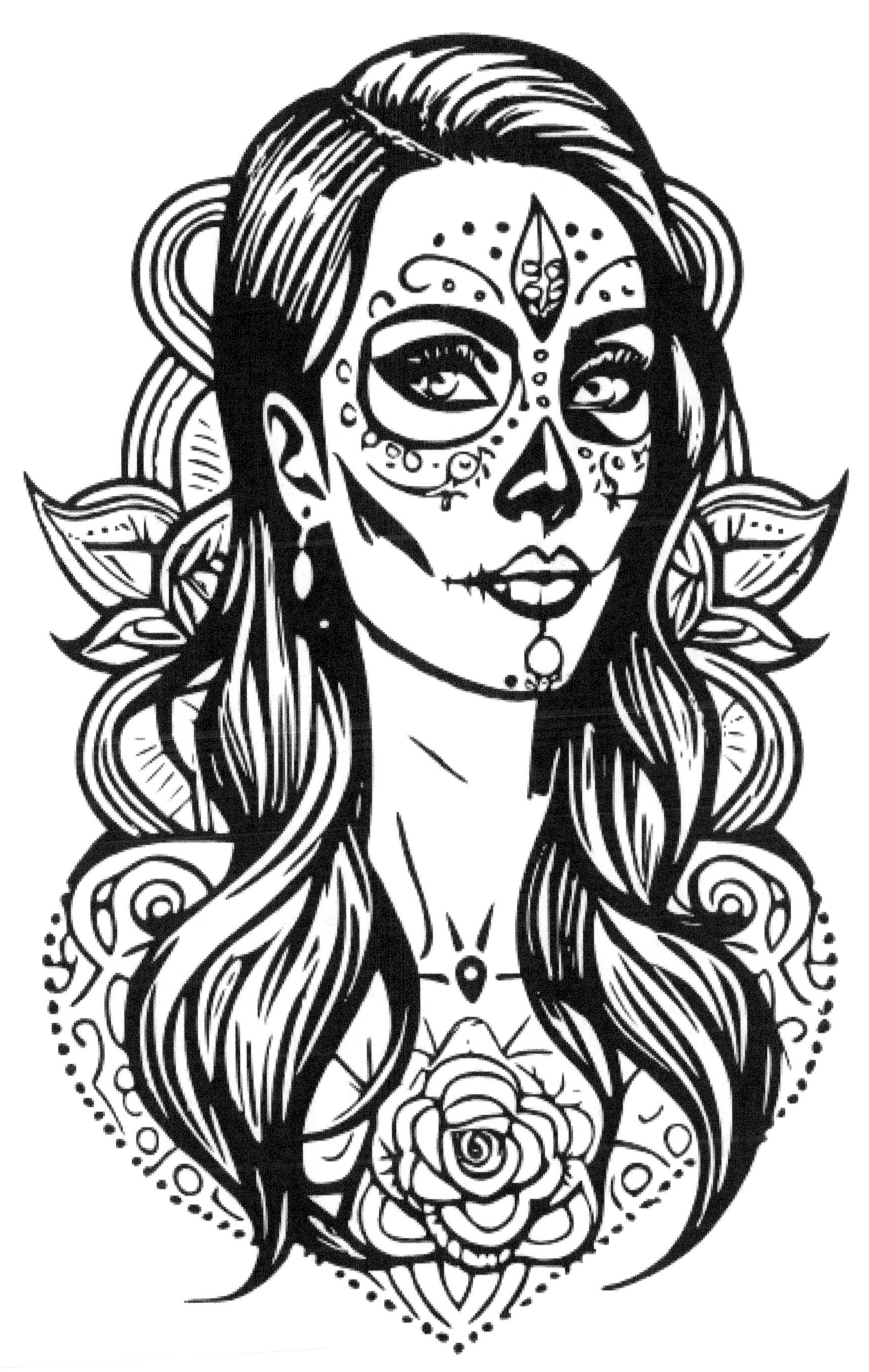

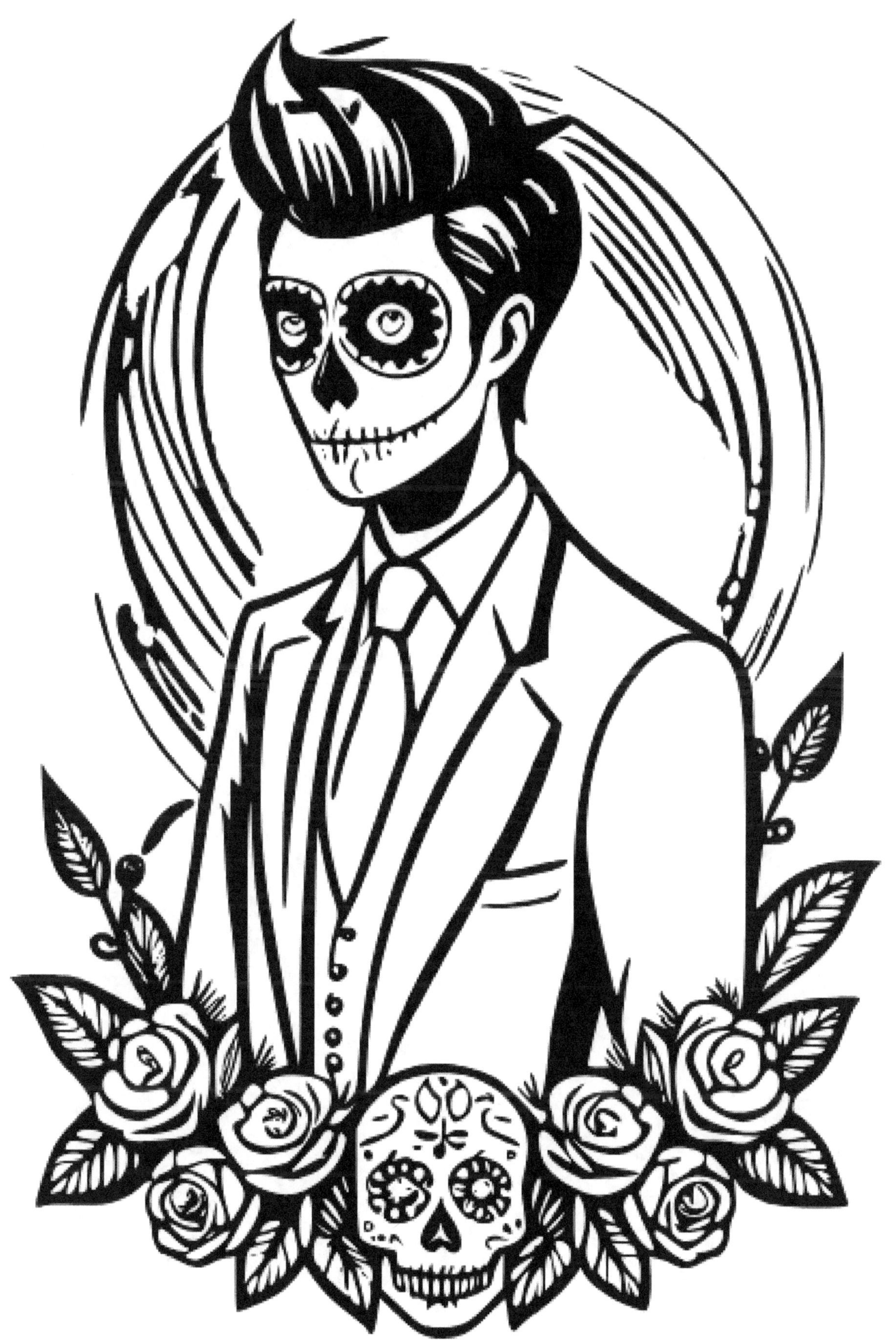

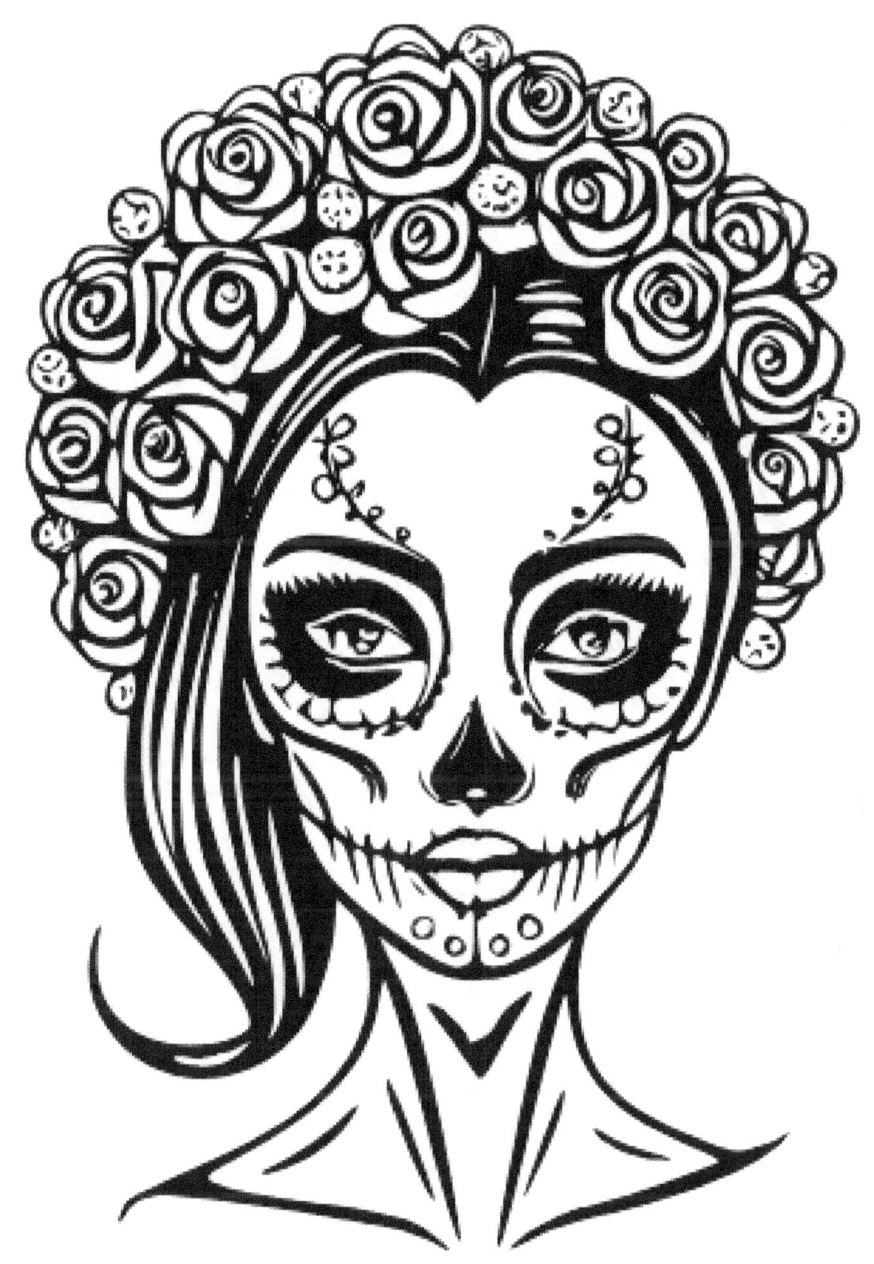

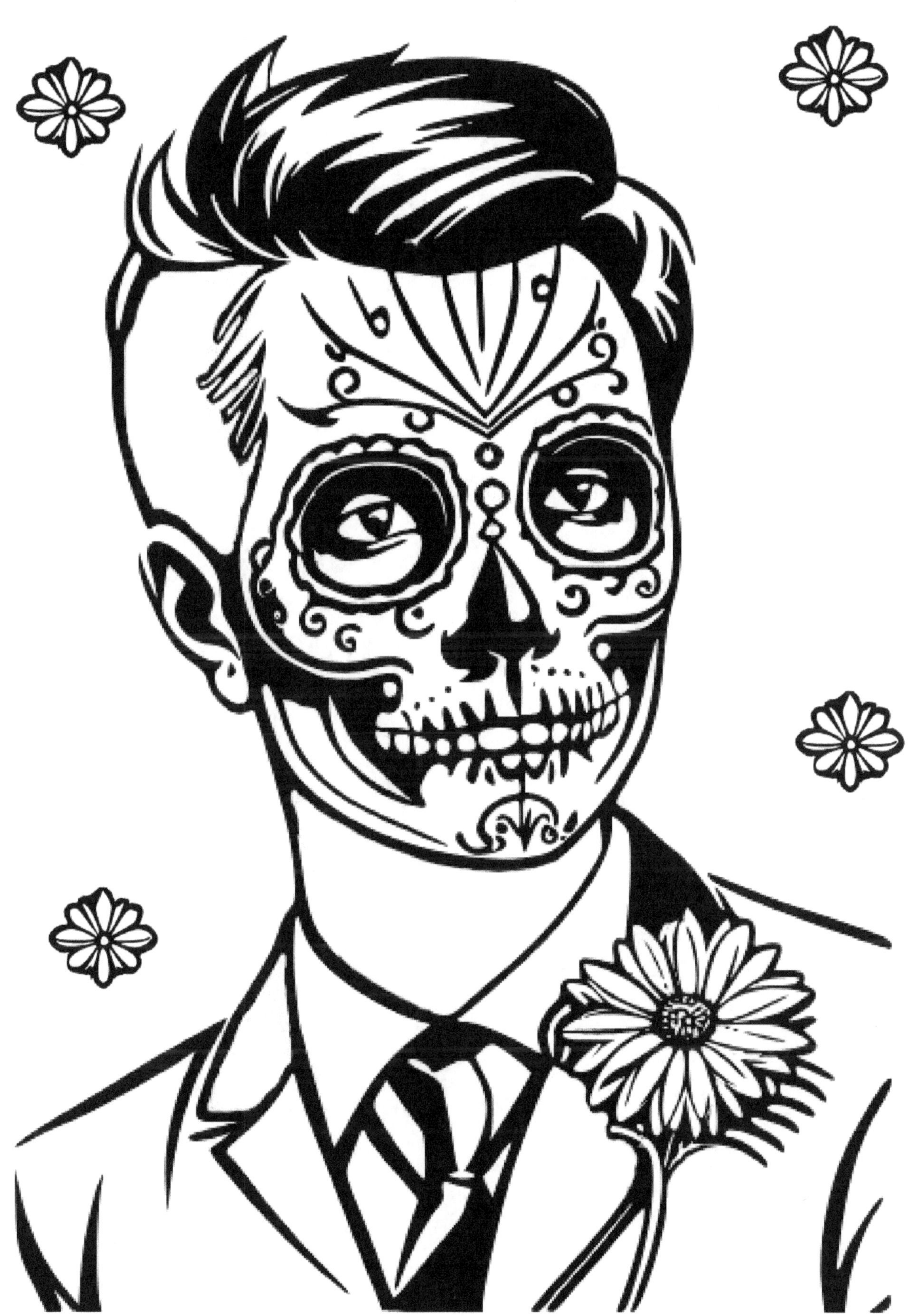

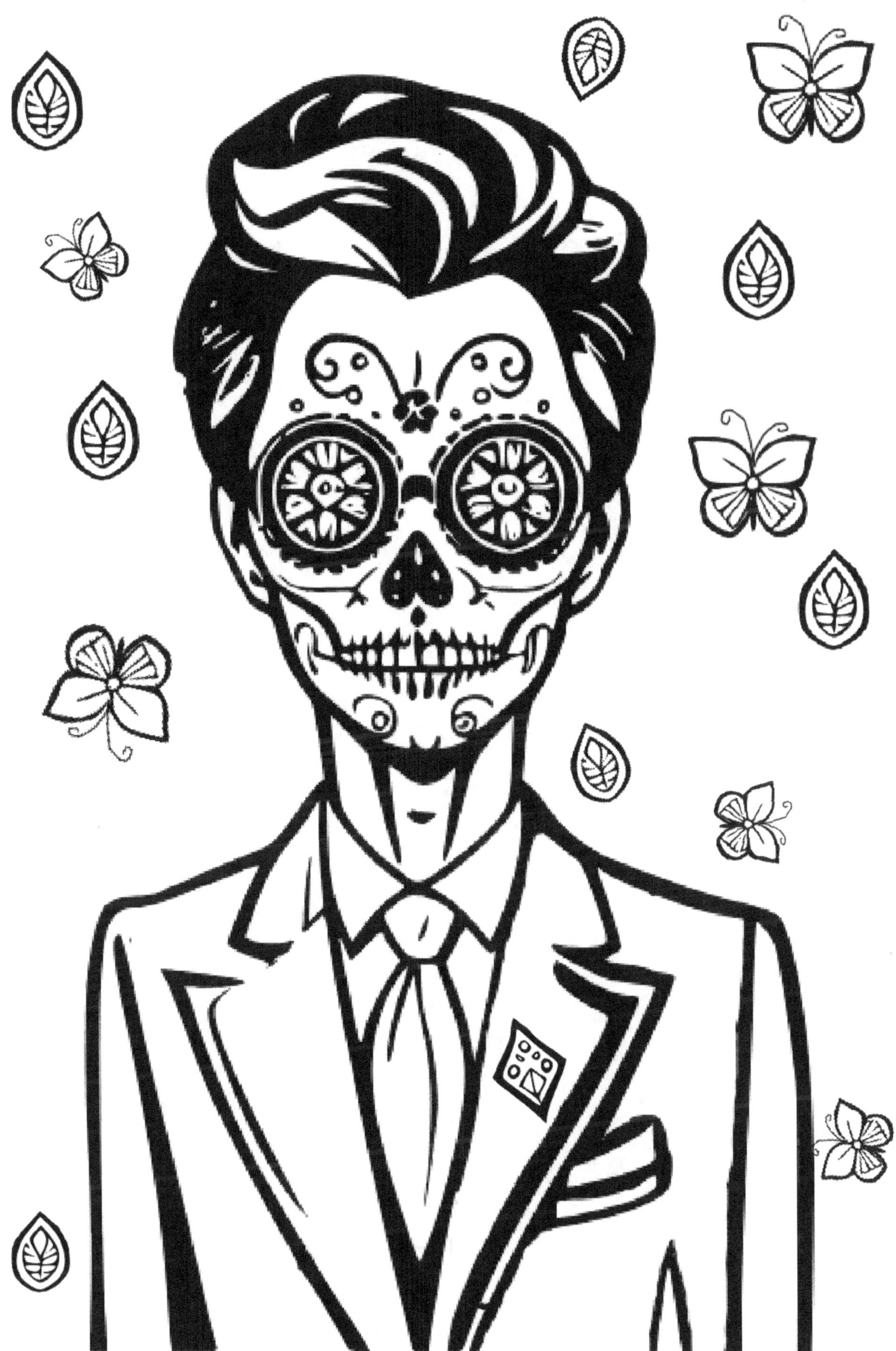

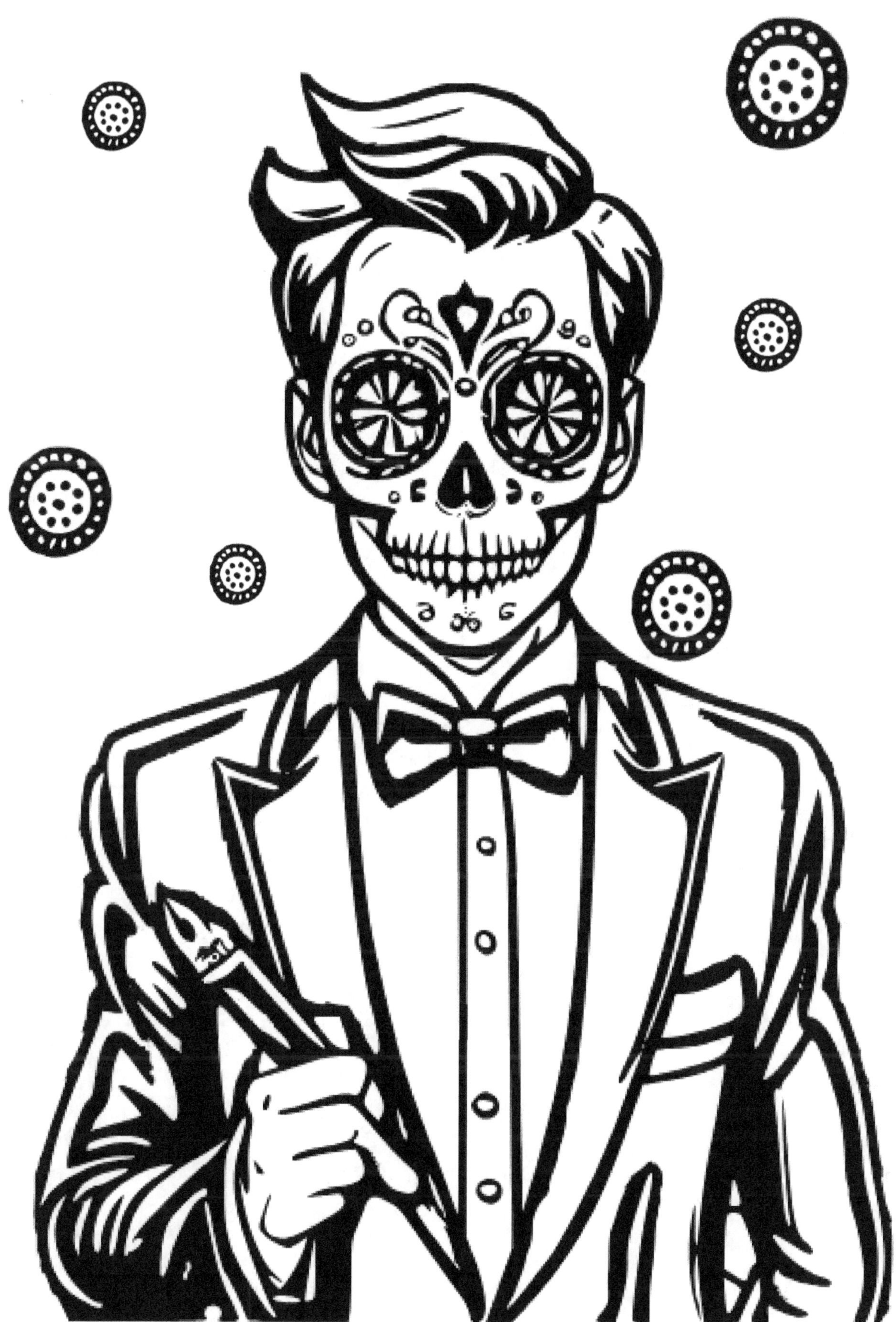

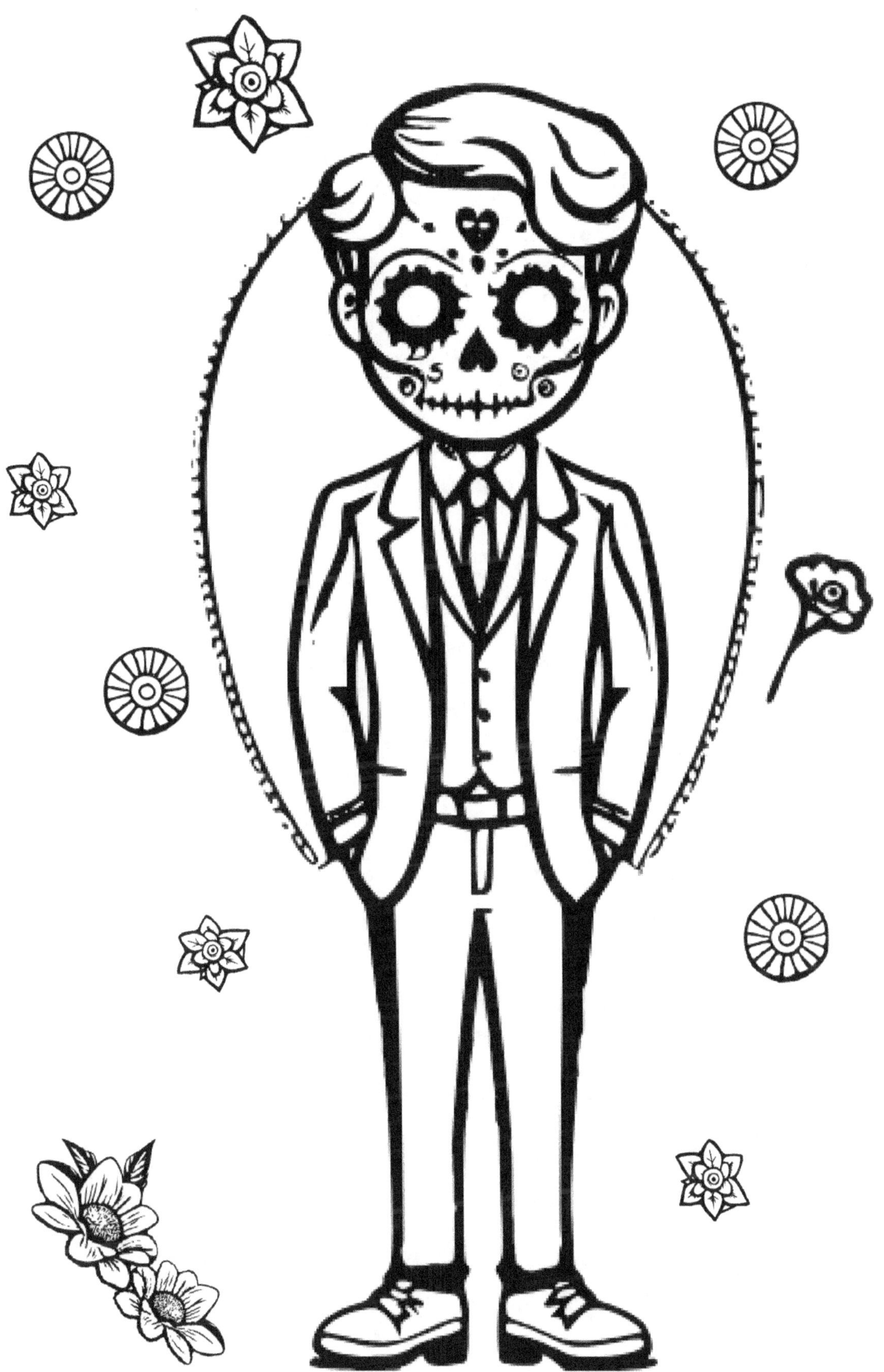

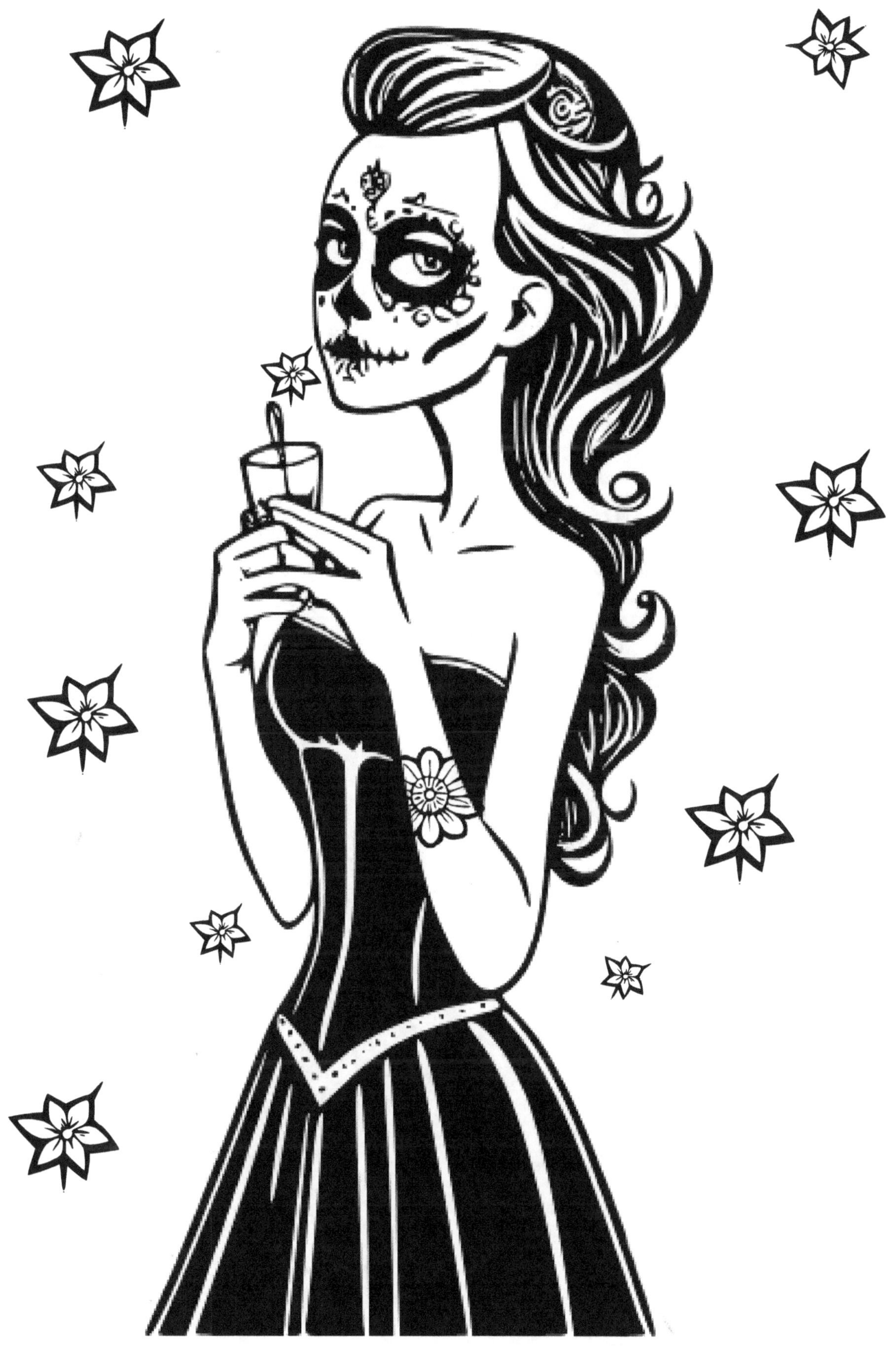

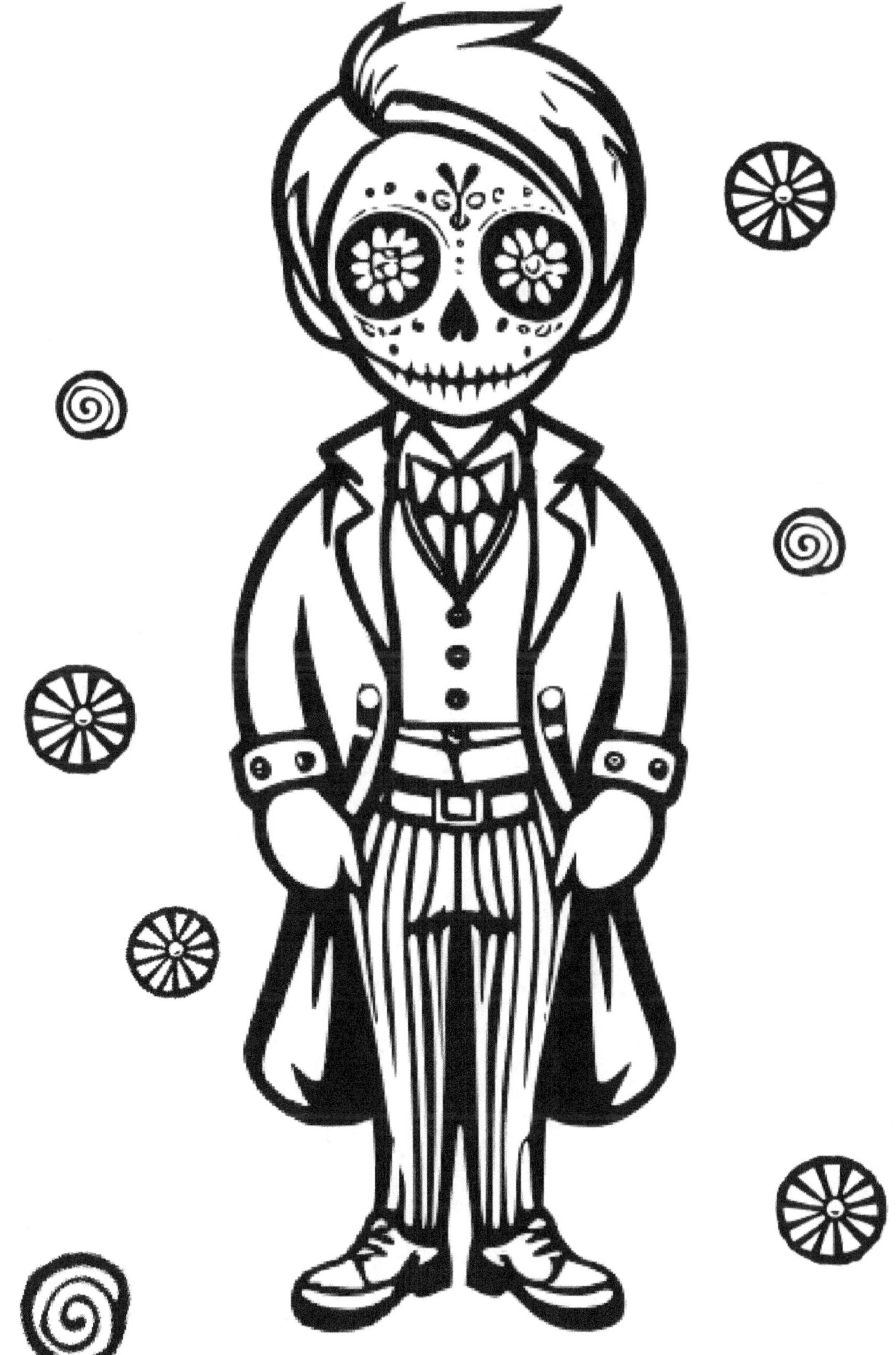

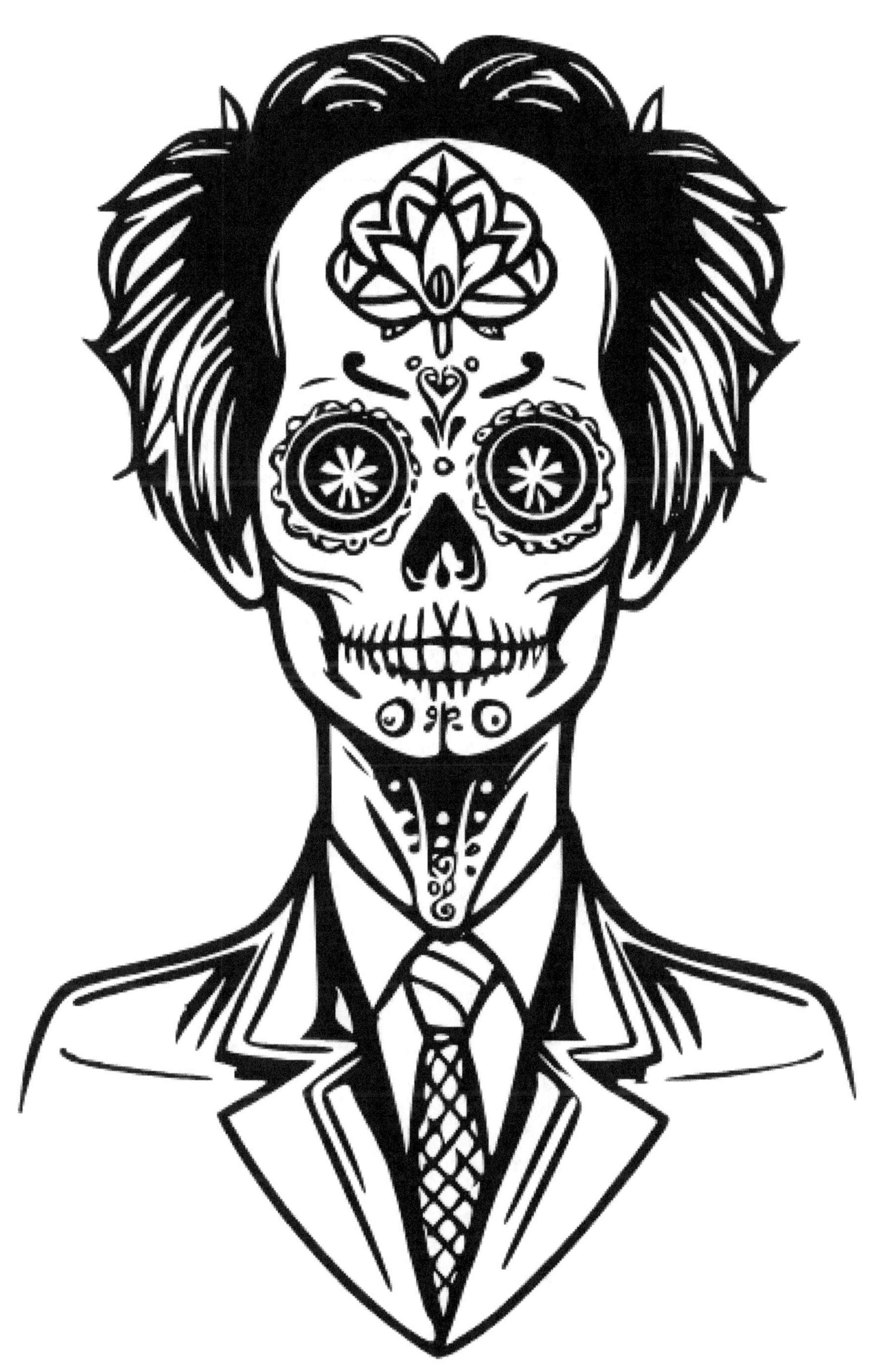

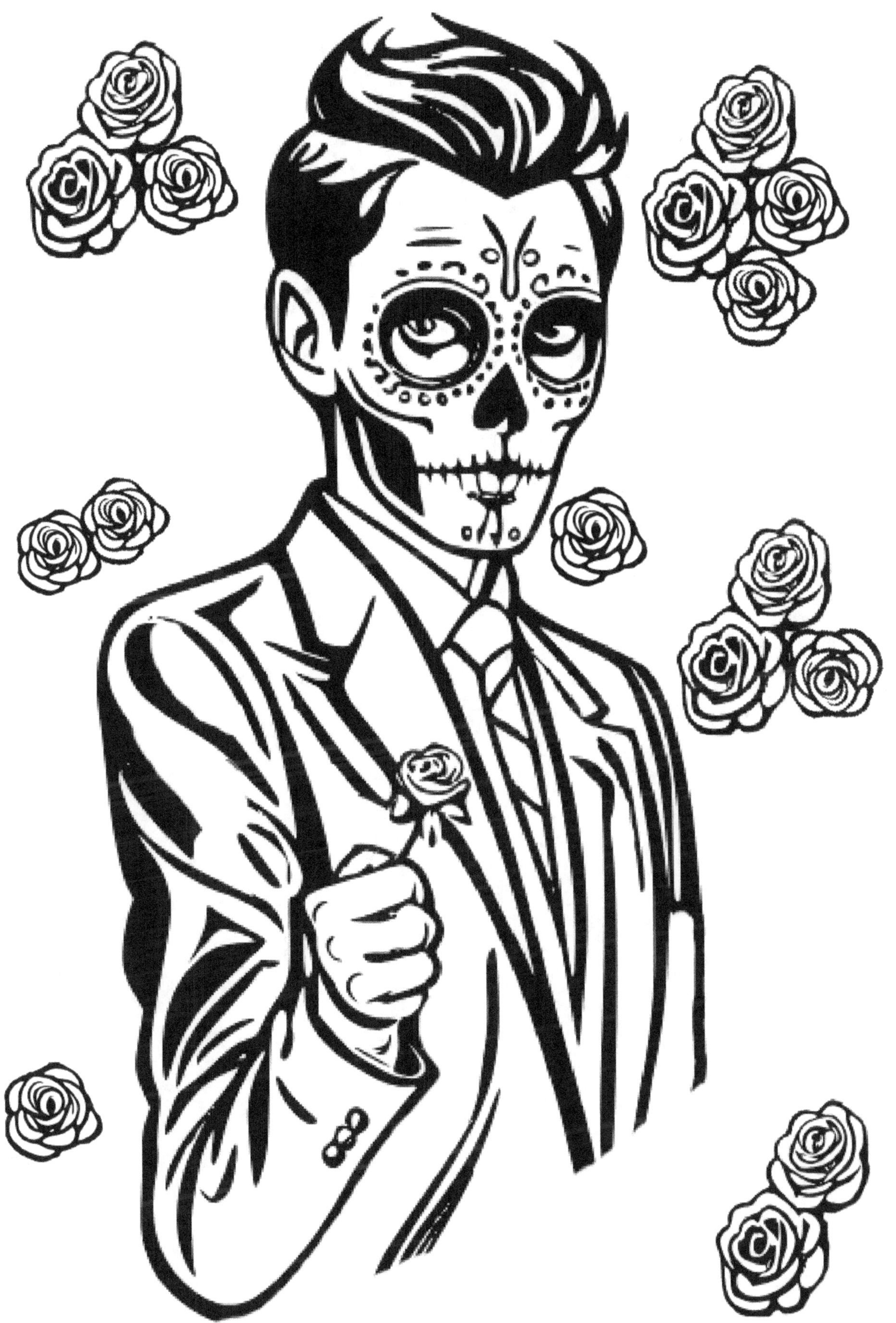

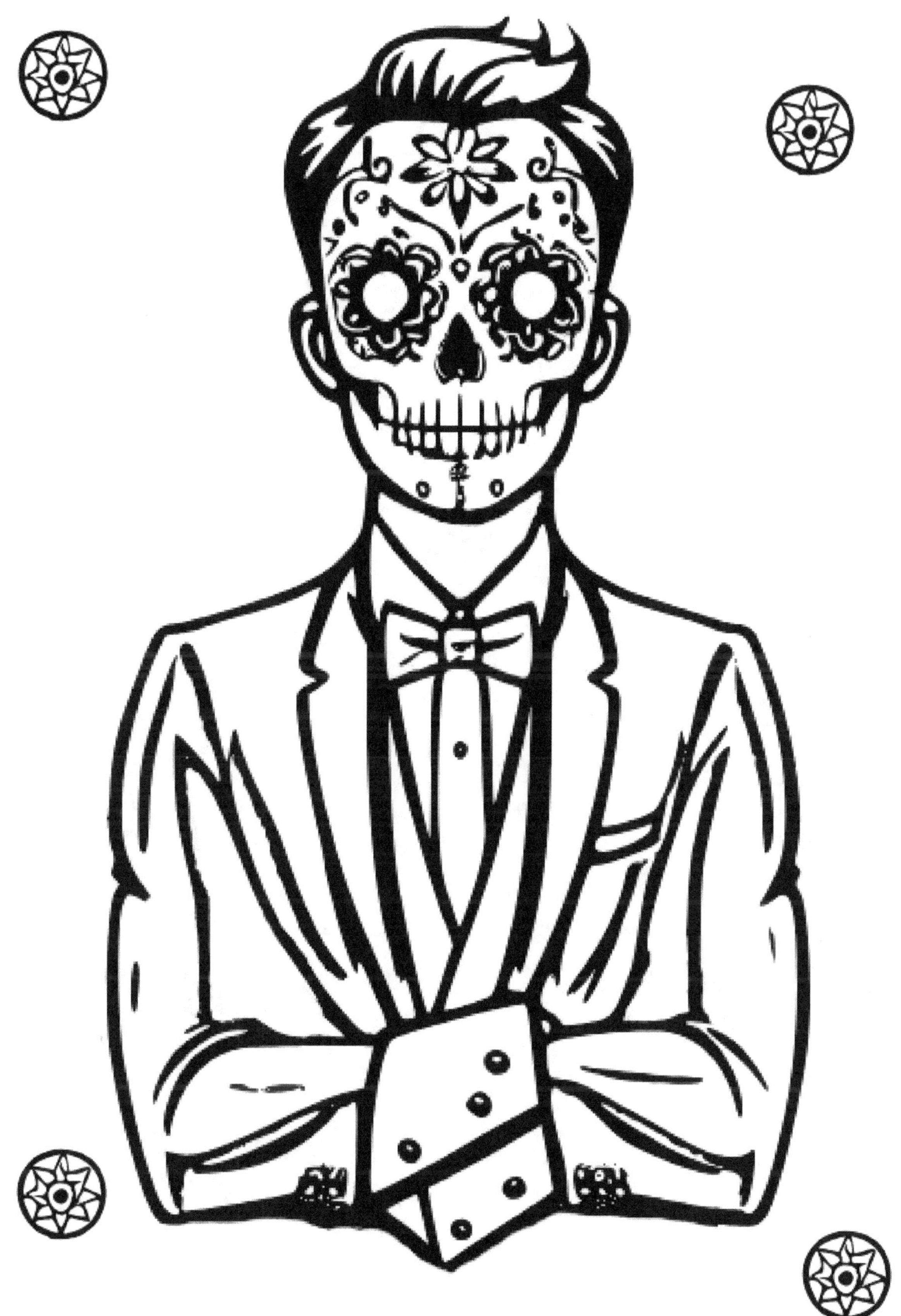

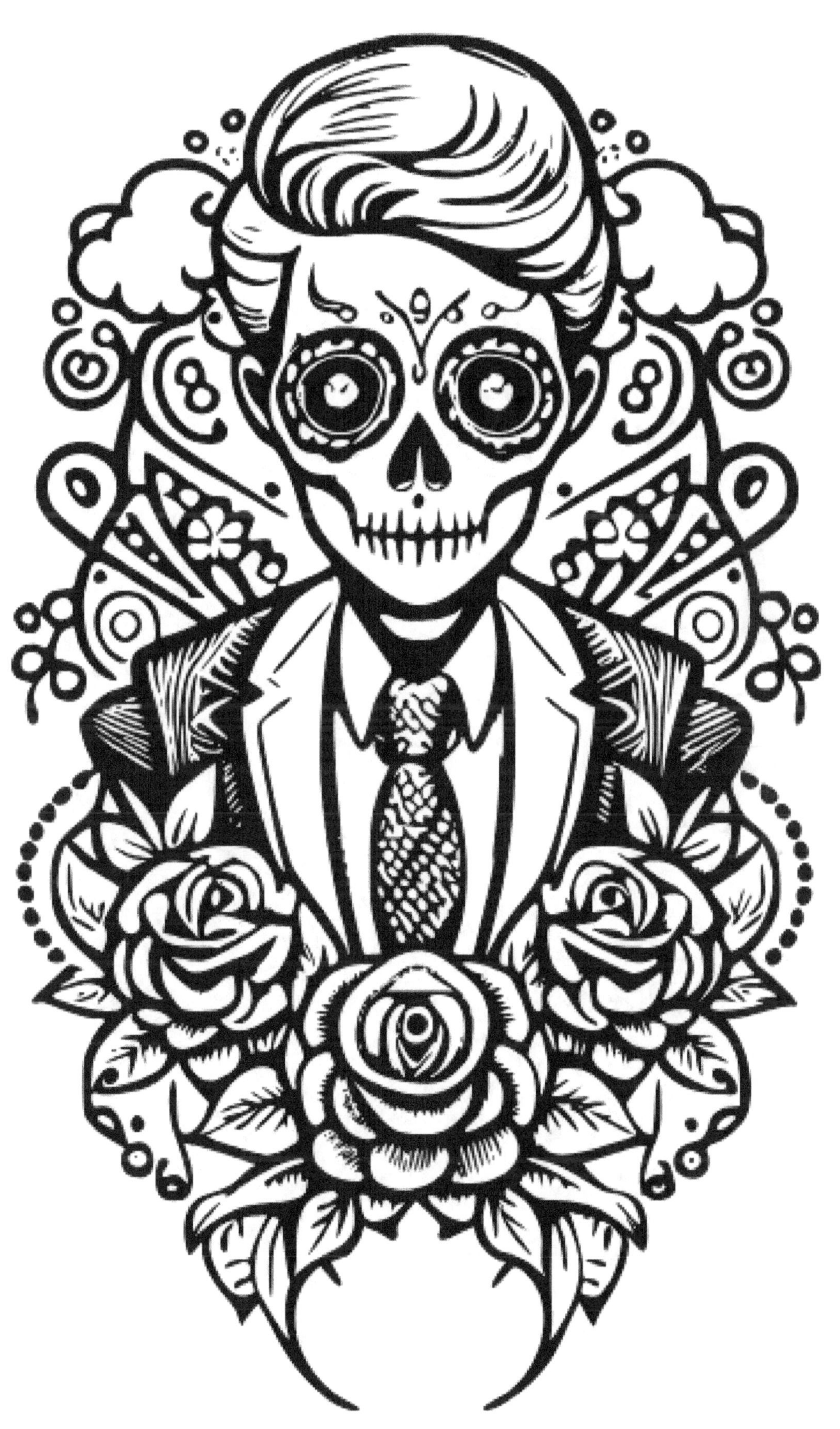

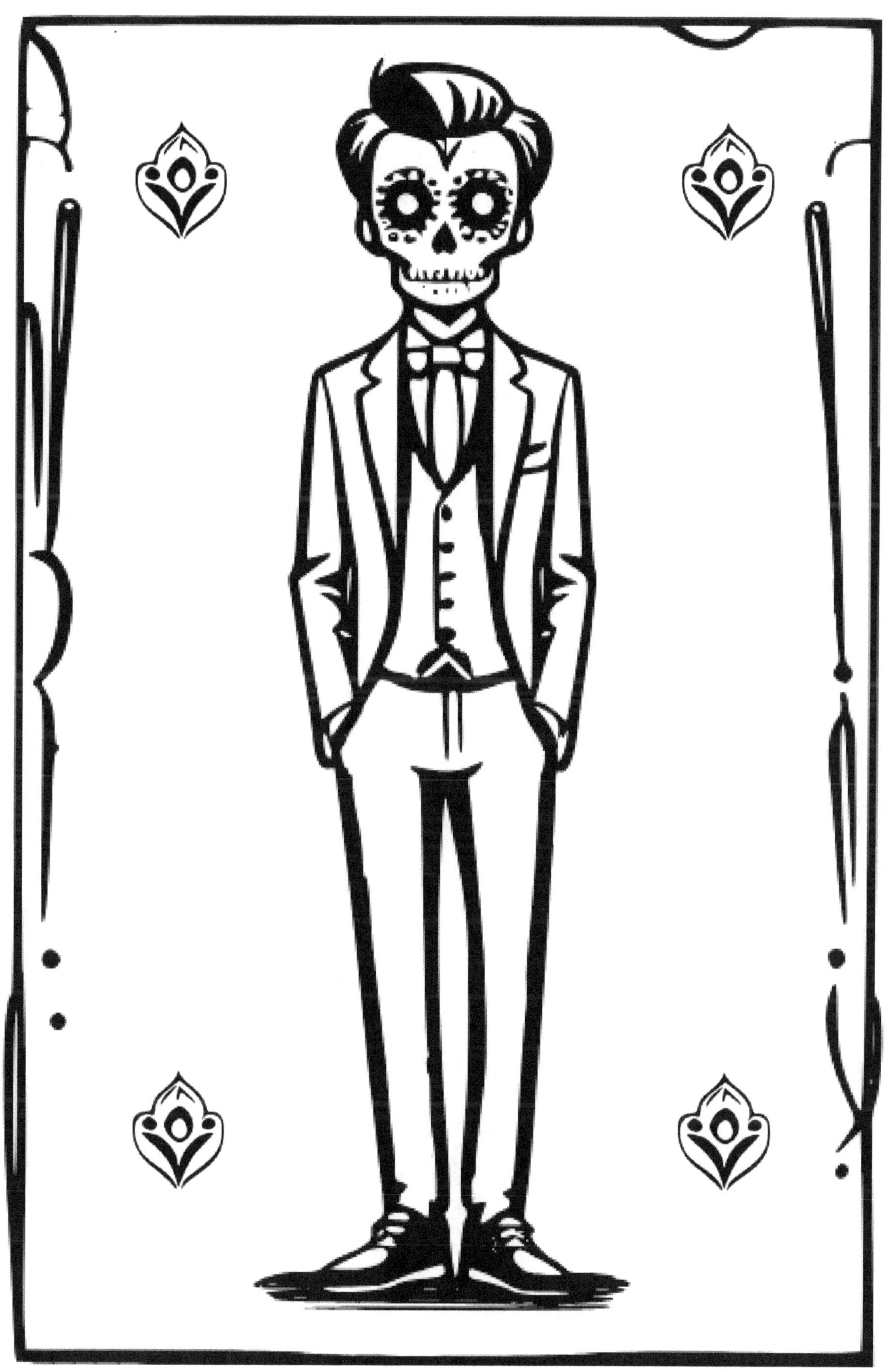

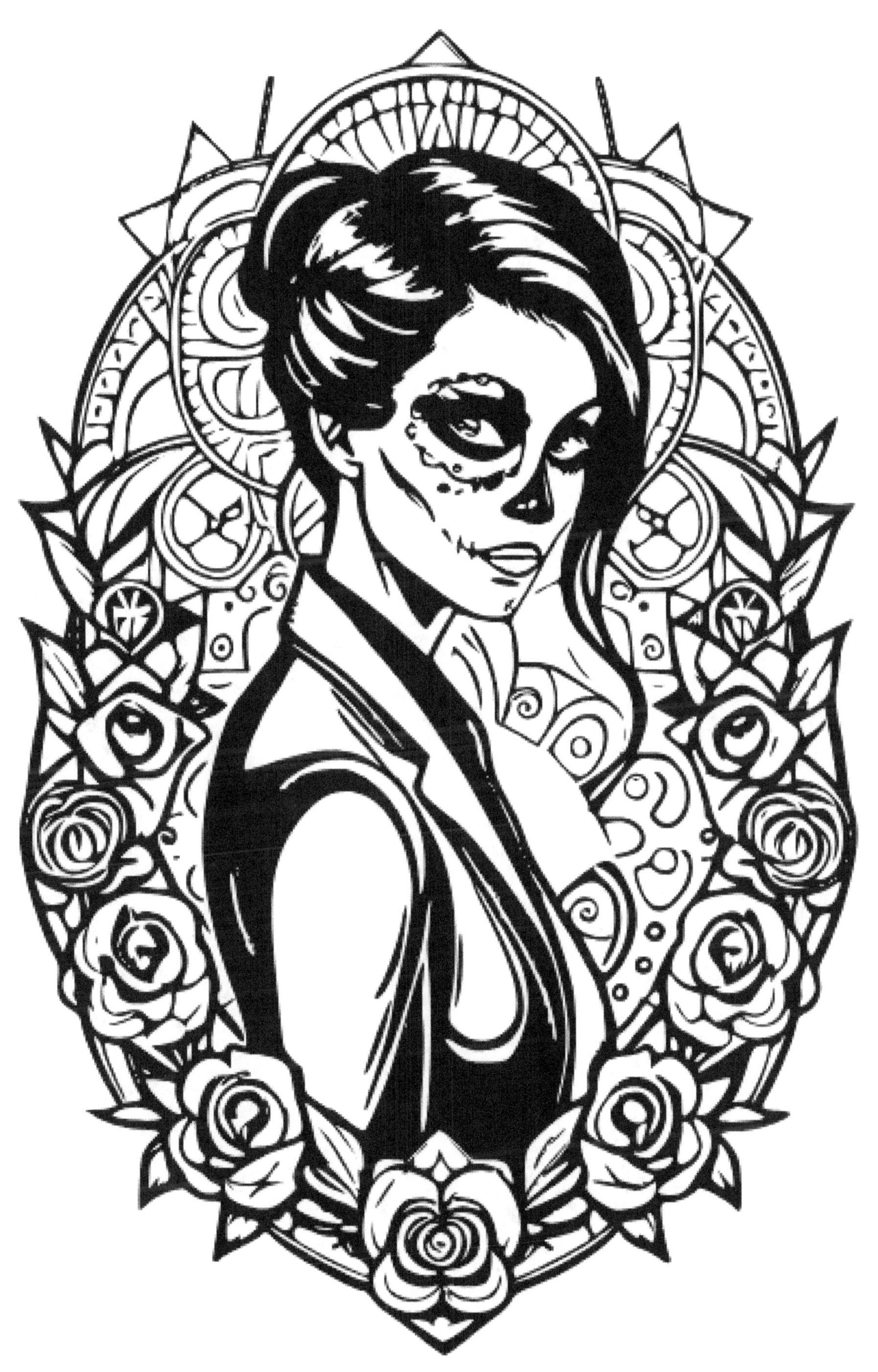

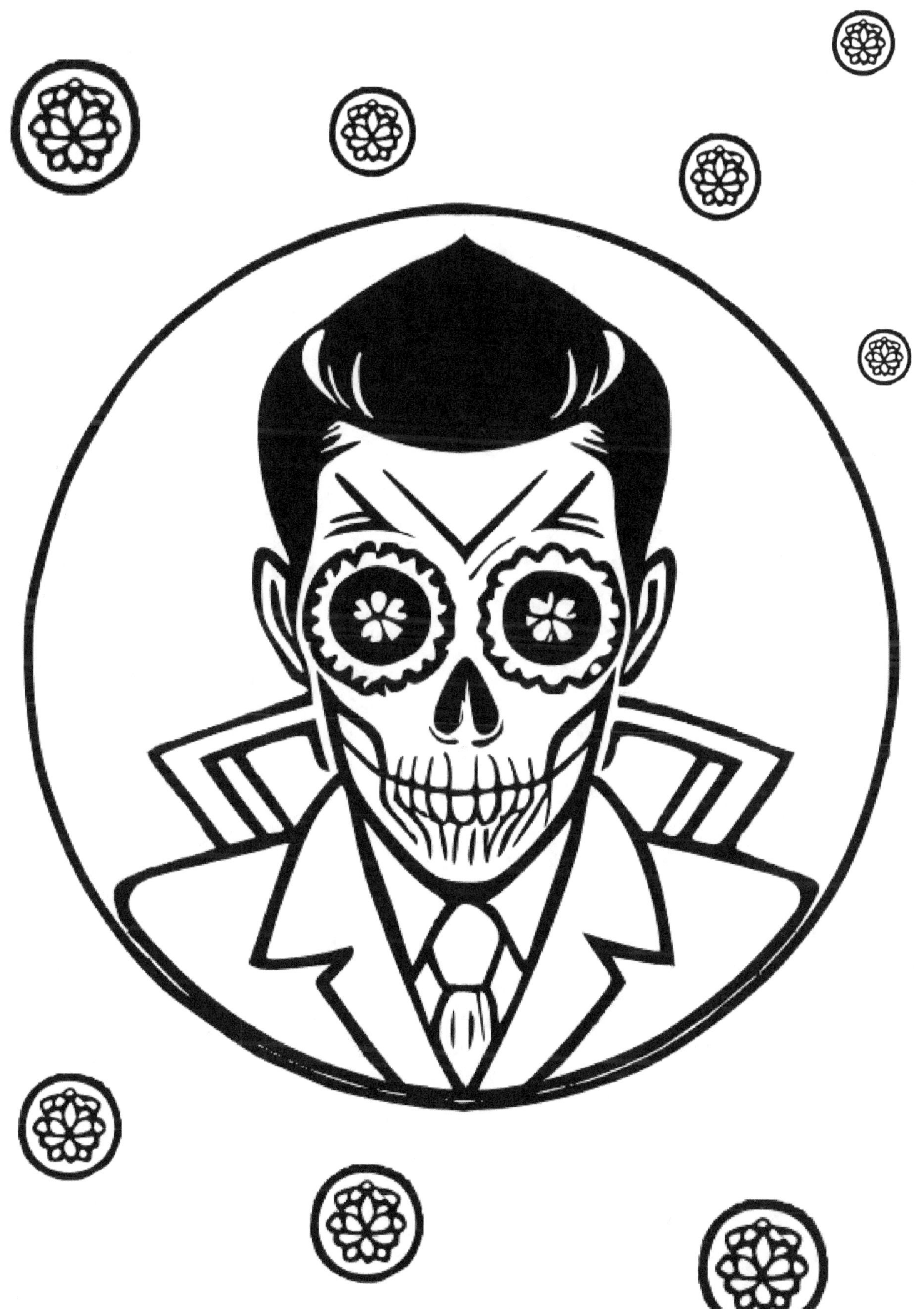

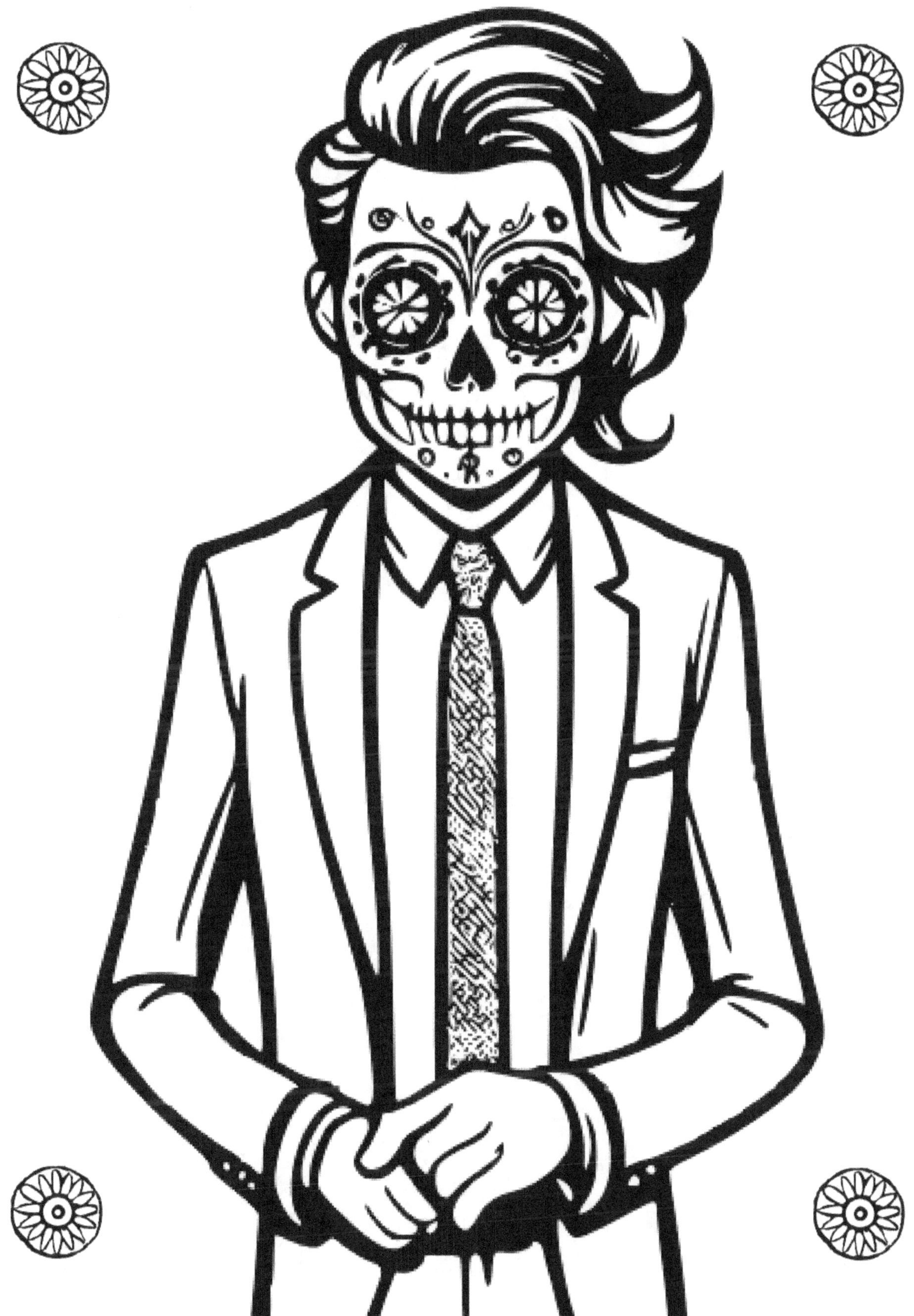

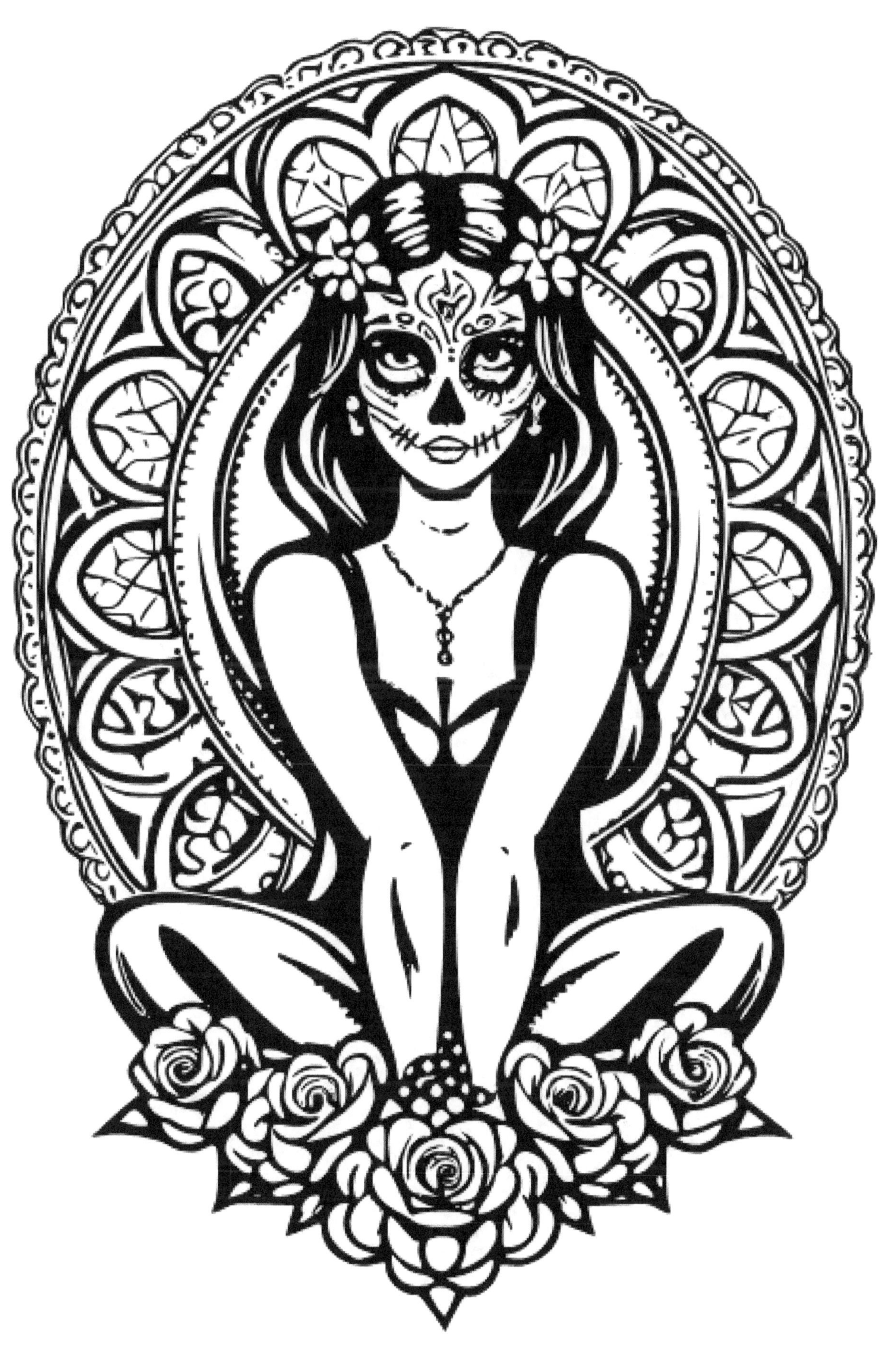

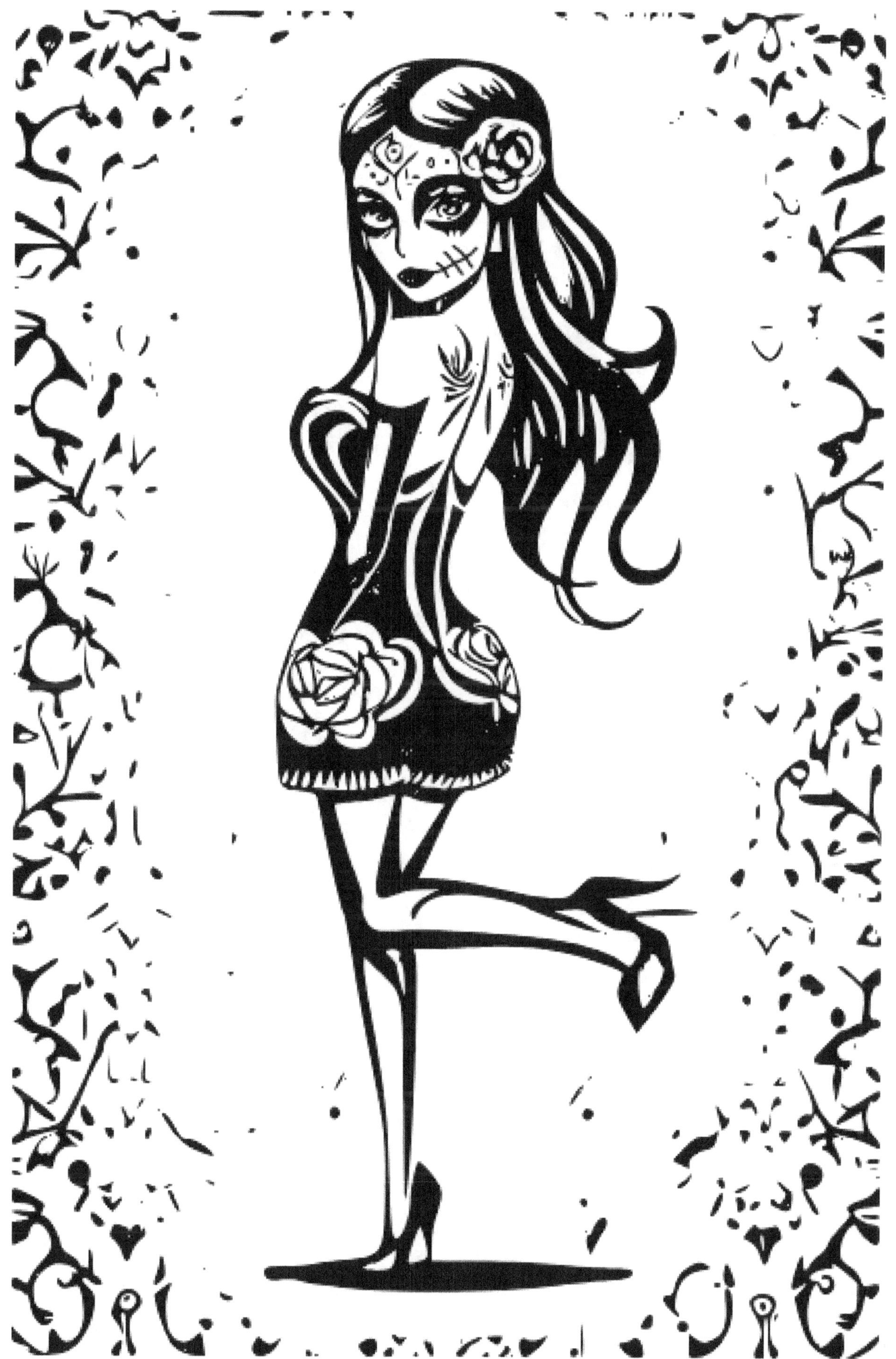